M000006476

Be the Light that You Are

*ten simple ways to transform
your world with love*

DEBRA LANDWEHR ENGLE

HAMPTON ROADS

Copyright © 2019

by Debra Landwehr Engle

All rights reserved. No part of this publication may be reproduced or transmitted in any
form or by any means, electronic or mechanical, including photocopying, recording,
or by any information storage and retrieval system, without permission in writing from
Red Wheel/Weiser, LLC. Reviewers may quote brief passages.

Cover and text design by Kathryn Sky-Peck
Cover art iStock.com
Typeset in Centaur

Hampton Roads Publishing Company, Inc.
Charlottesville, VA 22906
Distributed by Red Wheel/Weiser, LLC
www.redwheelweiser.com
Sign up for our newsletter and special offers by going to
www.redwheelweiser.com/newsletter.

ISBN: 978-1-57174-849-2

Library of Congress Cataloging-in-Publication Data available on request.

Printed in Canada
MAR
10 9 8 7 6 5 4 3 2 1

Contents

 # Acknowledgments

Over the past several years, I've had the joy of gathering with extraordinary people twice each month to study *A Course in Miracles*. The students in those classes have become my friends and teachers, and this book exists because of their thoughtful, heartfelt questions about what it means to live a spiritual life. I thank them for their wisdom, courage, and example.

Thank you to the team at Red Wheel/Weiser, including Greg Brandenburgh and Jane Hagaman, for giving me the time and guidance to fully develop this manuscript. Special thanks, too, to Eryn Eaton, who has been a source of inspiration and delight in bringing this book to the world, and to the production staff for elevating the meaning of every page through an inspired design.

To my agent, Stephany Evans of Ayesha Pande Literary, a huge thank you for being a staunch supporter, voice of wisdom, and friend.

And to my husband Bob, who stands beside me through the long days of writing and editing and cares just as much about my work as I do, I send love and gratitude for our life together.

And, finally, thank you to the spiritual guides and beings who remind me every day that we all have a light within. I am truly blessed.

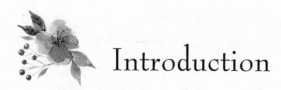 # Introduction

Not long ago, a student in my *A Course in Miracles* class asked an important question: "How can I stay friends with people who want to gossip all the time when I don't want to do that anymore?"

A couple of weeks later, another student asked this question: "I want to join a protest march, but I'm not sure how to do that without getting angry and upset."

And before long, this question showed up: "My cousin, who is black, was stopped on the street in her town by a man who told her to 'go back to Africa where you belong.' I wasn't there when it happened, but if I had been, I'm not sure what I would have done. I believe in love, but how could I have been loving at that moment?"

Even though the three questions look different, they're alike at their core because all three stem from the same inquiry: How can I stay true to my spiritual principles when I'm faced with challenging situations?

In other words, how do we move from having a spiritual practice to practicing our spirituality?

You may find that it's relatively easy to find inner peace in the quiet of your home, in prayer, and with the comfort of your spiritual guidance. But then a driver cuts you off on the freeway. Or you find your kids' dirty clothes on the floor. Or you get a surly response from your spouse after a lousy day.

At some point, we have to get up from our meditation, blow out the candles, turn off the soothing music, and use our voices, our hands, and our feet. We're made for action. So how do we live according to our beliefs? How do we help make this world the peaceful place we want it to be?

That's what this book is about: What to say. What to do. And how to extend the light that is you—no matter what situation you're in, who's in the room, or how much your fear-based ego mind wants to distract you from inner peace.

Is it possible? Absolutely.

Is it simple? Yes.

Is it easy? Not always.

That's why this book is designed to give you a foundation for understanding yourself and the world in a new way, as well as actual words and actions that you can use in everyday situations.

We all need a little coaching—especially when the world supports our fear-based thoughts instead of our inner light. This book will help you bridge the divide between where you are now and where you want to be, showing how you can stand in the middle of conflict and chaos and transform your world with love.

⌇

Has there ever been a time when we *didn't* think the world was insane? Probably not, but the intensity of craziness seems to increase day by day because we're constantly exposed to every form of ego fear.

Even if that fear didn't show up on our phones, laptops, and twenty-four-hour news cycles, it would seep into our awareness. You can unplug your TV, but you can't unplug from the collective consciousness.

We all have a tremendous opportunity to see that drama as a call for love—a plea for help—and then answer that call. In our own homes, communities, and places of work, we can quiet the chaos one conversation at a time.

The ten principles in this book will show you how to take action that's aligned with love, not fear, and how to speak with a voice that reflects the highest part of who you are rather than participating in anger and blame.

Some of the teachings may seem basic. For example, "Don't judge others. Respect diversity. Say you're sorry." All of these are excellent admonitions. But what does it really mean to not judge others? What's required in each one of us to make that possible? Does respecting diversity mean putting up with differences in other people, or does it start with respecting the diverse parts of yourself? And is it helpful to say you're sorry when you're doing it with clenched teeth?

Maybe the reason we don't always live according to our principles is because we don't fully understand what they mean, the foundation on which they're built, or their value in reminding us who we are. Hopefully this book will give you a deeper understanding.

Along the way, you may also find principles that turn your beliefs upside down or challenge ideas that you've held all your life—ideas that are supported in this fear-based world.

For instance, what if detaching from a conflict is the best way to show you care? What if the most compassionate thing you can do is *not* buy into someone's pain? What if trying to protect yourself actually makes you weaker?

That's why *Be the Light that You Are* is more than inspiration. It's a handbook for bringing meaning and understanding to events in your personal life and the lives of the greater whole, helping you move from bitterness and divisiveness to true peace.

I've written this book so that each principle builds on the ones before it, with practical examples demonstrating what they look like in everyday life. You'll see the cumulative impact as you read and put the ideas into action. But be gentle with yourself. There's a wealth of information here, and it's not meant to overwhelm. Incorporating these principles into your life is about practice, not perfection.

It's important to note that I've drawn these principles from *A Course in Miracles,* along with other teachings. This is not a Christian book or a Buddhist book or a Jewish book. It's a book for humans. It's about the higher ideals that govern us all, no matter where we live, what we do for a living, the color of our skin, our sexual orientation, our age, our occupation, or whether we worship and where.

Having said that, every principle in this book depends on a belief in a higher power. I use different names for that power, such as God, Source, and Divine Spark. In my mind, those names all stand for the same thing: the Creator, who is not defined by a particular religion or theology.

As a result, it may seem as though this book excludes atheists or agnostics, but that's not my intent. If any of the words for a higher power get in your way, substitute the word "Love" instead, and our beliefs will find common ground.

A couple of practical notes: Some of the examples in this book are based on stories I've heard or situations I've witnessed. Where necessary, I've changed names for confidentiality, and I've created composites of different people's experiences.

Also, on a few occasions, I use this wording: "Ask for your fear-based thoughts to be healed" or "Please heal my fear-based thoughts." Those statements come from *The Only Little*

Prayer You Need, one of my previous books. Reading about the prayer is certainly not a prerequisite to *Be the Light that You Are*, but it can add depth if you'd like to know more.

I hope *Be the Light that You Are* will serve as a primer, a reference, and a guide. The principles will help you step into your own power as an agent of change and peace, as long as you lift them off the page and into your everyday life.

So don't just read this book and then put it on a shelf. Keep it with you. Use it. Mark it up. Fill it with sticky notes. Read it before you go into potentially contentious situations. Return to it if something in your life feels "off." Know that you can have a voice. You can take action, and this book will prepare you to do that as the light that you are.

The only thing this book requires is a willingness, no matter how small, to believe that we *can* live without constant drama, violence, and conflict. If you think your life and the world will always be broken and nothing will change, try suspending that belief just for a moment and let some light flow in.

By the time you finish reading, I want you to feel a sense of comfort and hope. I want you to be equipped with practical ideas and responses you can put in place right away. And I want you to know that your words and actions matter. You don't have to be a public figure, run for office, or start a nonprofit to move this world forward in a positive way. With small adjustments in your everyday life, you can bring higher ideals into our fear-based world. And you'll know how to do that as the light that you are.

Your ability to respond with love is possible because you *are* that love. You *are* that light. If that's something you don't believe or completely embrace just yet, that's okay. Because that's exactly where we'll start.

one

Be the Light

Within all of us, there's a light that shines like a lantern's bright flame. We may call it love, divine energy, or an expression of our Source. No matter what name we give it, that light never goes out.

As we go through our lives, though, our self-doubts dim the sides of that lantern. The drama in the world adds its own layers of soot. And eventually, it's easy to lose sight of the flame burning within, forget how bright it is, or believe it was never there at all.

Fortunately, our forgetting doesn't change the brilliance of the light, but it can limit our ability to claim the truth about our very existence. In fact, by starting this book with "Be the light that you are," we're beginning with one of the most challenging principles of all.

It's the only place *to* start, though, because every principle in this book rests on the solid foundation that you are the light. Without that, the layers of other teachings would teeter on shaky ground.

We've spent generations building our world on a fear of who we are. That's why, to build a better world, there is no place to begin but the truth.

When I was a little girl, I knew there was something more than this world of houses to live in and Monopoly games to play and bicycles to ride. On some level, even though it wasn't conscious, I knew that we each had a soul, a spirit.

Our dog, Pepper, and all her puppies had souls. The sycamore tree I climbed in the front yard had a soul. The fireflies we caught in Mason jars with holes punched in the lids had souls.

The word "soul" means different things to different people, but I mean it as a spark of light, a mysterious but animating energy that brought us to life and gave us the ability to feel, care, and experience.

I knew this light came from a source beyond me, and that we all embodied it. And it was so much more than how we looked or what we wore or how we acted.

Our gruff old neighbor across the street had it. So did my teachers—the ones I liked and the ones I didn't. So did Billy, the boy in my class who talked with a lisp and was the target of other kids' jokes.

3

And although I lived in a homogenous neighborhood in a homogenous state, I knew that the people of other colors and countries that I saw on TV had it, too.

Knowing there was light in everyone was not a special gift on my part. I'm guessing that as a child, you knew this as well. Hopefully you still do. But often the knowledge that we are the light—a light of goodness that's as divine as the power that created us—gets wrung out of us, and fear of not being enough takes its place.

That's why it's so important to start with this foundational belief and restore it, remember it, and embrace it—no matter how tentatively at first—so you can transform your world with the truth of the light within.

⁓

The idea that you are the light may seem radical. But references to being the light show up in every major religion and spiritual teaching.

❀ *A Course in Miracles* says we are "the light of the world."

❀ The Buddha said, "Be your own lamp, seek no other refuge but yourself, let truth be your light."

❖ Matthew 5:14–16 says, "You are the light of the world . . . let your light shine before others, that they may see your good deeds and glorify your Father in heaven."

Each of these quotes alludes to the truth that the Spirit/ Creator/Higher Power who created us is divine love, and so are we. In other words, the Spirit/Creator/Higher Power who created us is not broken, sinful, bad, evil, or incomplete. And, as Spirit's progeny, neither are we.

No matter what your life circumstances, your connection with God means you are entitled to abundance, well-being, peace, and joy. That's the starting point, not the destination. You don't have to go out and find what is already in you.

You may resist this idea. You may remember the words to an old hymn that proclaims your sinfulness or Bible verses that portray an angry and vengeful God. You may feel that you're unworthy of such a divine inheritance.

You may immediately think about all the mistakes you've made, all the ways you've hurt people or stood by and watched as others were hurt. You may point to Hitler or Stalin or school shooters as examples of evil. You may start to build a case for why you can't possibly be the light, and even why it's blasphemous to think that you are.

But that resistance, those arguments for "evidence" of brokenness, can't alter the truth.

It's like the total eclipse of the sun. For those few moments when the Earth casts a shadow and midday becomes dusk, it looks as though the sun has dimmed. But, of course, the sun is the same as ever. A momentary blockage doesn't change the fact that it's still there, as powerful and brilliant as it has always been.

We, too, have momentary blockages that seem to cast a shadow on our light. Those barriers could be fears and insecurities. Judgments of others and ourselves. Feelings of guilt and shame. Stories about hatred and war.

And then we focus on those barriers. We judge them. We think about them over and over. We listen to others who reinforce them for us. And before you know it, we've forgotten the light within and believe that our blockages define us, and there's no escaping them.

"Fear has been taught for so many centuries, by so many learned people, that it has become institutionalized."

In fact, these fears have been taught for so many centuries, by so many learned people, that they've become institutionalized in our schools, our laws, and our governments.

And it's true, there's no escape—because we don't need one. We simply need to remember our light rather than our fear, and we'll see that we've been free all along. At that point, everything else in our lives will start to align.

That's why it helps to remember when you were little and could see the pure light in yourself and others, before it became stained with fear. And if you can't recall a time of seeing the light, that's okay.

This book will help you remember.

How do you remember that you're the light? How do you take a lifetime of indoctrination to the contrary and start to embrace truth rather than falsehoods? How do you get to the point at which you can look in the mirror and say, "Yes, I am the light" as easily and naturally as you say, "I am a mother" or "I am a teacher" or "I am a social media manager"?

First, it's important to distinguish between *what* you are and *who* you are. Throughout your life, you've probably been asked the question "Who are you?" in a number of different ways—on forms, applications for school and jobs, or when you meet someone new.

The answer to "Who are you?" typically goes something like this: "I'm Marilyn Garcia, and I have two children. My husband and I have been married for sixteen years. He's a contractor and I'm a bookkeeper."

This provides a quick snapshot of your life. A word picture that allows us to see you with your husband and children or at work.

But how often in your life has anyone asked, "*What* are you?" The question may seem odd.

"What do you mean, '*What* am I?' A vampire? A spy? A backup singer in a rock band?"

The answer to that question is the great equalizer because it's the same for everyone: You are the light.

This truth comes from a level beyond personality, identity, or circumstances of birth. It's the level the Founding Fathers recognized in writing the Declaration of Independence. The statement, "All men are created equal" makes that document not just a charter for a new nation, but a sacred affirmation for humankind.

That's the level on which we're called to live. That's why remembering the truth about the light that we are is so essential to our peace—both individual and collective.

~

But what if you don't feel like the light of the world? What if you've been taught that you're a miserable sinner? What if you look around and don't see much light or love in your life?

Your current beliefs and life circumstances may feel deeply ingrained and hard to shake, but I can assure you that once you say, "I want to know myself as the light of the world, as the child of Spirit that I am," you will open the door to a new vision of yourself. Be willing to suspend your disbelief and entertain the idea for just a moment. That's all it takes to start remembering.

Some people have erected their entire lives on the idea of brokenness, helplessness, or victimhood. For them, the truth can be disturbing because it threatens the structure of their lives and all the fears that have built them. So the first steps toward remembering the light that you are need to be gentle, yet persistent. For instance . . .

Envision opening a door and seeing light flood in.

Take a moment each day to sit in quiet and express thanks. Smile at someone, as simplistic as that sounds.

Consider the stories you've told yourself about who you are. Pay attention to how many of those stories are based on your "shortcomings" or "failings." When you become aware, you'll likely see that those stories, no matter how deeply embedded they may be, don't fully explain who you are or what you're about.

Listen to the voice deep within—maybe long buried and faint—that says, "I am more than my fears. I am more than my mistakes. I am more than my shame. There is light within me I have not yet seen."

A part of you will fight hard to keep from going inside and seeing that light, but there is nothing to fear. As you remember the light that you are, you'll expose your old structures and beliefs for what they are: simply a story. Because you've lived with that story for a long time and it feels like home to you, nothing will be gained by making yourself feel homeless. So be patient and gentle with yourself. Don't try to dismantle the structure all at once.

What if a voice in you is saying, "Why should I believe that I'm the light of the world when I've been taught exactly the opposite?"

If that's the case, take an honest look at what your beliefs have built in your life, because everything we experience comes from what we think about ourselves. Often a belief in sin or brokenness creates a deep chasm of shame and guilt, and you start believing that's who and what you are.

Think of all the gay men and women who marry because they believe their sexual orientation is "sinful," then live their lives in shame and fear of being found out. Think of the adults who abuse children as a punishment for their "sins." Think of the millions of lives lost in wars that have been fought because another country or culture was "sinful."

Teachings about sinfulness sometimes lead to mercy and compassion, but they also can lead to a distrust of God, yourself, and the world. This can make you feel alone, cynical, and rudderless because you always wonder if you deserve to be loved. And even when you're surrounded by love, you can't let it in.

So do this one simple thing: Change the word "sin" to "fear." For example, instead of "I'm sinful," change it to "I'm afraid." Instead of "That school shooter is sinful," he is "overwhelmed by fear." And instead of "This world is sinful," it "feeds our fear." This language reflects the fact that we're not broken, we've simply forgotten who and what we are.

When you remember, you're likely to feel a deep sense of coming home. You may have wandered down a lonely path for a while, but now you can trust the welcoming light within.

———

We've been trained to think that claiming our gifts and grandeur equates with self-importance. But knowing you're the light of the world doesn't mean that you're a braggart or that you think you're more important or special than others.

There's a big difference between saying, "I'm more important than anyone else" and "I'm important because I'm a child of God—and everyone else is, too." The latter statement is not arrogance. In fact, *A Course in Miracles* says just the opposite is true. If God made us to be the light of the world, who are we to deny His creation?

*"If God made us
to be the light of the world,
who are we to deny
His creation?"*

So what do you have to do to be the light? Nothing. As *A Course in Miracles* says, there is nothing you need to do, say, or prove to be the light that you are.

There are no tests, no training, no certification. You don't have to accomplish it or dream it because you are—simply by virtue of being—the light.

Imagine a majestic oak tree in the middle of a park. Children come and sit under it for shade and shelter. Families take pictures of it because they admire its beauty. Couples talk about how much they love that oak tree for all the joy it brings to their lives.

Does the oak tree do anything? No, it just stands, rooted, being the tree that it is. And by sharing its innate gifts, it invites others to come and experience love.

That's the perfect metaphor for the light that you are. You don't have to be right. You don't have to be the best. You don't have to do anything except stand in your grandeur as a child of God. As you can imagine, this has the power to change everything in your relationships and interactions with others—and with yourself.

As you claim the light that you are, it helps to honestly ask yourself these questions:

- ❀ Do I try to please others so they will like me?

- ❀ Do I avoid conversations because someone might judge me or I feel like my voice doesn't matter?

- ❀ Do I question my value or try too hard to prove myself?

- ❀ Do I overlook, take for granted, sabotage, or dismiss the gifts in my life because I'm looking for the next thing to make me happy?

- ❀ Do I blame someone else for my troubles?

- ❀ Do I judge others for looking different or acting in ways that are foreign to me?

If you answer yes to some or all of these questions—and I'm guessing 100 percent of us do—it's an indication that you've forgotten the light that you are. This doesn't mean you "failed." You just need to take a moment and remember what you are once again.

So, every time you become aware of these thoughts and actions, stop yourself and then do something simple: Stand in a pose of grandeur for thirty seconds—feet firmly planted, shoulders relaxed, hands outstretched with palms up. Ask for the light to flow through you and be directed wherever it needs to go.

Let yourself be the oak tree with nothing to prove.

And, as you remember what you are, give thanks for the light within you that never goes out.

⌒

While you needn't do anything to *be* the light, here are four steps that will help you *remember* the light that you are.

Pay attention to what you tell yourself. Make a commitment to say one loving thing to yourself each day. As the days pass, increase the compliments to yourself so you're seeing and acknowledging the light within on a regular basis. You won't believe the flattery at first, and that's okay. But keep going until it feels more natural and you're better able to claim the truth.

Spend time in your heart every day. Nowhere is your light more easily witnessed than in your caring heart. Spend time daily in gratitude for your blessings, sending love to the people you care about, and asking a power greater than yourself to extend love throughout the world on your behalf. The more you feel the light within you, the more you will trust that this is your true nature.

Bring more beauty into your life. When you start feeling frustration, anger, anxiety, shame, or guilt, focus on beauty instead. Buy yourself a bouquet of flowers or spend the day at an art museum. This may not seem relevant, but it will start training you to see the light rather than the darkness. Beauty is effervescent. It lifts you up and restores your vision to something you value, which will help you remember the value in you.

Imagine the light within you. In your mind's eye, focus on a spot just above your navel, and see the light as a candle, lantern, or open flame. Imagine the glow of light that it casts in a circle around you. See that light growing brighter and the circle of light growing as well. Imagine it touching everyone around you. Ask yourself how you feel as you visualize this. Know that any peace or blessings you feel are real, and that as your light blesses others, you are blessed, too, because you're remembering the light that you are.

~

What does it look like in real life to know you're the light? Here are three examples.

1. Your husband had a bad day and comes home in a foul mood. He's never physically abusive, but lately his frustration at work has carried over into dinner conversation, and he has barked at you and the kids without apology or noticing the toll he's taking on everyone.

Without claiming yourself as the light of the world, you might snap back or absorb his negativity. Eventually, you might question your relationship. "Maybe this is my fault. Maybe he doesn't love me anymore. Maybe he's having an affair." In other words, you would end up doubting and diminishing yourself. When you don't claim your value as the light of the world, it's easy to take things personally and allow yourself to be confused—and potentially abused.

When you claim yourself as the light of the world, you can see that the best way to spread your light is to balance compassion for others with compassion for yourself. In this example, compassion for your husband might sound like this: "It looks like things are rough at work lately. Let me know if you'd like to talk about it." And the compassion for yourself could sound like this: "I'm sorry you're going through a rough time, but it's not acceptable to take it out on me or the kids. Thank you for doing whatever you need to do to improve the situation. I know you want to do the right thing for all of us."

You don't take responsibility for his emotions, and you don't get swept away by them. You don't turn the situation into more than it is, take it personally, or make assumptions about what's wrong. You simply stand in your light, affirm your own inner peace, and allow yourself to shine.

2. You go to a craft fair and visit the booths of local artisans. You're especially drawn to the photography exhibits because you dream of starting a photography business someday. In fact, you have pictured yourself with a studio of your own ever since you were little.

Without knowing you're the light of the world, you might dismiss the value of your dream. "I could never compete," you tell yourself. "Being a professional photographer is just a pipe dream. Better not quit my day job." Then you go home from the fair feeling dejected and try to talk yourself out of being upset.

But when you know you're the light of the world, you can trust that your work has value and your childhood dream has a purpose. As a result, you speak to some of the photographers at the fair and ask how they got their start. You can feel the stirrings of joy within you—especially when one of them invites you to attend the next local photography club meeting—and you go home with a sense of possibility and next steps. By reaching out for help and trusting that you'll receive divine support, you reinforce the innate light within and give it the freedom to shine.

3. You see a homeless person on the street with dirty clothes, greasy hair, and missing teeth. Without knowing you're the light of the world, you may look at that person with derision and blame. In your mind, you might say, "You're a blight on society. Why don't you get a job?"

But when you know you're the light of the world, you can look at that person and witness a light within him as well. "I see the truth in you. No matter what your circumstances, you are the light you were created to be."

Even if no words are spoken, your acknowledgment will touch you and the homeless man as well. Trust the truth in this. Light beholds light, and every remembrance of light for yourself extends the possibilities for others.

⁓

Being the light means:

- ❁ You have a purpose that has nothing to do with your job or the many roles you play in life.

- ❁ You're willing to turn many of your old beliefs inside out and upside down and see them from another perspective.

- ❁ You're not alone because you're connected to something greater than yourself.

- ❁ Compassion, kindness, abundance, and well-being are your natural state, so you needn't do anything to earn or deserve them.

❀ You don't have to prove your value to anyone because your value is an innate state of being.

❀ When you combine your light with the light of others, powerful and wondrous things can happen with less effort.

❀ You're not a victim in a random universe.

❀ Like you, everyone on the planet is more than their bodies, opinions, and circumstances.

❀ You feel powerful and supported. Your heart opens up, and you feel more compassionate and less guarded.

❀ You become aware of opportunities to bless others every day. You allow yourself to be used for good, knowing your light can only increase the light in others.

❀ When you need answers and support, you trust that you'll find guidance by turning within.

- You embody the ultimate strength and invulnerability, knowing that the ever-changing external world can't touch the steadfast strength of who you are.

- The light that you are is made manifest in your connection to Spirit. Every time you ask the higher power to guide your thoughts, words, and actions, you bring more light to the world.

- No matter how much you forget or deny the light within, that light never goes out. The path to peace is always just a remembrance away.

Above all, remember this: No matter what has happened to you, no matter what decisions you've made, no matter how old, educated, prosperous, fit, or happy you are, you are the light. No exceptions.

If you're sitting in prison reading this, know that you are the light. If you just yelled at your kids and grounded them for the next month, know that you are the light. If you feel alone, you are still the light. If your ex-spouse just got remarried and all the hurt from your divorce has resurfaced, you are still the light.

If you've got a chronic or terminal illness, you are still the light. If you're addicted to alcohol or drugs or food or work or sex, know that you are the light. If you cheated on your taxes, you're attracted to your husband's best friend, you haven't been to church in years, or you just binged on a plate of nachos, you are still the light.

Forgetting you're the light undoubtedly got you where you are now. That was your only real issue. It's not that you're sinful or bad or broken or don't have willpower. You just forgot or believed something different from the truth. You don't have to be redeemed. You simply have to remember what you are.

When you combine your light with the intentional use of your mind, you take enormous steps toward peace.

And how powerful is that mind?

Ahhh. Great question. That brings us to the next principle.

two

Apply the Power of
Your Mind

nce you know and understand that you are the light, you can know and understand your mind differently than before—and put it to better use.

We see the creative power of the mind when we build a business, remodel a bathroom, write a poem, or fit an entire week's worth of clothes in a tiny carry-on suitcase.

You use it every day to manifest your desires and communicate with the world—even if you do have to rely on a ten-year-old to figure out your smart phone.

But how well do you really know your own mind? How adept are you at using it to create what you want rather than what you don't? How much do you respect it as the greatest tool you'll ever have in extending your light into the world? Do you see yourself as the master of your mind, rather than your mind holding mastery over you?

To understand the true creative power of your mind and how you can use it to spread your light in the world, we need to start with one basic teaching: We are all of two minds.

Intuitively, we've always known this. We've seen it represented as the angel who sits on one shoulder, representing your conscience, and the devil on the other shoulder, representing your mischievous or "evil" side.

But those two sides are not separate from you. They're as much a part of you as your big toe or your beating heart. Those minds have worn a lot of labels, but for our purposes, we'll refer to them as the lower mind or ego self, and the higher mind or higher Self.

The easiest way to explain the difference between them is this: The lower mind is based in fear, and the higher mind is based in love and light.

The ego mind feels guilty and alone, seeing everyone as separate bodies and engaging in a cycle of attack and defense. The higher mind knows it's connected to Source, and that nothing can separate us from the love of God, our Selves, and one another.

The ego mind covers up the truth that you are the light with insecurities, self-doubt and feelings of guilt and shame. It's the reason we resist the truth that we are the light of the world. It's the part that believes we're broken rather than whole.

The higher mind, our true Self, knows that we have a light that never goes out. It is unaffected by global politics, family squabbles, daily drama, and bad hair days.

The ego mind constantly scans the landscape for relationships, approval, and opportunity.

Our higher mind knows we never have to go out and look for love, success, abundance, or joy. We *are* those things. They flow through us as the light that we are.

It's essential to understand that we *all* have both minds. They're part of our existence as human beings. We all express love, and we all project fear.

Some people become so rooted in fear that they take violent action against others or build empires on what's considered evil intent. But they're not innately evil. They simply are using their ego mind to obliterate any memory or acknowledgment of the light within, believing this will make them more powerful. Of course, in the end, the light always wins because it endures, whereas anything based on fear ultimately fades.

The more you acknowledge who you are as the light, governed by and using your higher mind, the less you'll rely on your fear-based lower mind to control your outer circumstances.

When you understand this, you no longer abdicate responsibility for your thoughts to a devil that made you do it or sinfulness in your DNA. You realize anything that's hurtful comes from your fearful ego mind, and anything that's loving comes from your higher mind. You understand that only what comes from love is real. The rest is just rooted in a false belief about yourself.

And every single day, in every single moment, you get to choose which of those minds will do you and the world the most good.

Making that choice isn't hard. But living according to the decision you make takes practice and vigilance because your ego mind will always insist it's the right option, and the world will add its voice of fear to yours.

The good news is, even though your ego mind is noisy and tenacious, your higher mind is eternally patient. It's like a parent watching a toddler run in circles, knowing the child will burn herself out eventually and quiet back down into her true Self.

Because nothing—not even your ego mind—can permanently interfere with the light that you are.

Let's look at some essential elements of this principle.

You can become aware of the source of your thoughts. Once you do, it's not hard to distinguish between your ego mind and your higher mind.

First, pay attention to how your body feels. If it feels heavy or burdened, stressed or unwell, you're probably feeling the effects of fear-based thoughts. If you feel light and happy, relaxed and at peace, you're probably feeling the effects of a connection with your higher Self.

Second, are your thoughts about the past or the future? If you're thinking about the past, you may experience guilt, shame, remorse, or frustration over something you or another person did. If you're thinking about the future, you may experience anxiety or worry over a possible event or outcome that feels beyond your control, like health or money issues. These thoughts all come from fear.

Third, take a look at whether your thoughts lead to resolution and peace or to anger and frustration. Are they life-affirming or hurtful? Do you feel doubt or trust? Do your thoughts reflect an intention for the highest good of all? Or are they mired in fear that someone else is going to "win"?

In the end, the easiest way to tell the difference between your two minds is to ask this question: Do my thoughts make me happy and at peace, or do they make me agitated or depressed? You don't need to overthink your own thoughts. If you do, you can be sure your ego is involved.

"Move your awareness to your higher mind and feel the infinite love flowing through it."

You are not a victim of your mind. We can whittle our waist, build our muscles, improve our health. But when it comes to the mind, we often accept our fear-based thoughts without question, never entertaining the idea that fear is just one option.

The other option, of course, is your higher mind. It's the most powerful tool you have because it's fueled by Spirit.

When you align your mind with light and love, you think, speak, and act from the light rather than drama or uncertainty. This is the meaning of right-mindedness, and it's a stark contrast to the ego mind.

When you're thinking with your fear-based mind, your thoughts may be something like this:

❀ "That would be just my luck."

❀ "How come things always work out for everybody else but not for me?"

❀ "You can't depend on anybody anymore."

❀ "I need to figure this out."

❀ "Let me get this under control."

I once had an encounter with a stranger at a home improvement store that demonstrates this way of thinking. I was waiting for my husband, Bob, and entertaining myself by looking through the bargain shelves. A man nearby mumbled something to himself, so I looked his way.

"I was here last week and got four bags of rubber bands for forty-nine cents apiece," he said. "Now they're $1.19 each." He shook his head and, as he stomped off, he said, "A guy can't catch a break."

Apparently he forgot that he *had* caught a break the previous week when he scored four bags at a super-bargain price. But his ego was on alert, ready to catch the world taking advantage of him.

Have I done the same thing more times than I can fathom? Absolutely. We all have, because that's what our egos do. And does it have anything to do with rubber bands? No. It's just the ego finding the latest reason to say, "See? Things never go my way. I'm screwed again."

Why do we put up with such mental belly fat when we could use the fit part of our mind instead? Because we've forgotten the light that we are. Shifting to our higher mind reminds us of the joyful flame within.

Your mind is linked to all other minds. Even though we inhabit bodies with our own unique gifts and personalities, we're not distinct and disparate beings. We're united because we're all created by and plugged into the same Source. As the light, we are all connected to God, ourselves, and one another. You can't divide love or light.

Because of this, what you choose to think doesn't just impact *you*, it impacts *everyone*. This is why we need to be deliberate and careful in what we think, because we're constantly adding to fear or extending love, depending on which part of our minds we're using.

This is not something to dismiss or overlook in your life. It's the difference between a life well lived and one that's wasted or lived idly.

Whatever happens in the world, we need to see that we all contribute to it by the thoughts in our own minds. Instead of looking at war and shaking our heads with despair, we can look at that war and say, "I contributed to that with the anger in my own mind." When we see an act of kindness, we can say, "I contributed to that with the thoughts of love in my own

mind." When a school shooting happens? "We all did that."
When a cease-fire happens? "We all did that."

Think of it like the ultimate recycling program. Do you
want your thoughts to throw trash in a landfill or contribute
to a useful new invention that moves the world forward?
Wherever your mind is, your actions follow. So if you want
to do something different for yourself and the world, you've
got to think something different first.

Your higher mind is infinite. The ego mind may appear
infinite as well, but it's actually limited by its own boundaries
of fear and human experience. The higher mind is powerful
because it draws from the vast resources of spiritual
connection, beyond our human limitations. When you're
thinking and creating from the higher mind, you're thinking
and creating with the mind of God.

We may not be able to wrap our minds around infinity, just
as we can't imagine existence without space or time. But our souls
know infinity, and nature gives us reminders of it every day.

Look at the horizon or into the night sky, and you're
looking at infinity.

Gaze out over the ocean, and you see an infinite number of drops of water.

Imagine the air that you breathe every day and think about the infinite number of oxygen molecules that keep your body alive.

The infinity we witness in the external world also exists in our higher mind, and becoming more aware of that fact can help us utilize our higher minds more effectively.

If your higher mind has an infinite capacity for love, how much sense does it make to hold a grudge against someone and block the infinity with a simple grievance?

If your higher mind has infinite creative power, why would you keep it circling in the same groove of old patterns and ideas?

If your higher mind is a conduit for unlimited appreciation, why would you focus on lack rather than abundance?

When you apply your higher mind to any situation, you break free from the limitations of fear-based thinking and tap into light that has no boundaries.

What can you do to start using your higher mind more and your ego mind less?

Gaze inside yourself and see the vastness there. Because our brains are encased within our body, we sometimes put limitations on what they can do. But when you know your higher mind is plugged into an infinite source of creative power far beyond the body, there is virtually no limit. Do you want to travel to another part of the planet or the universe? Just imagine it in your mind and you're there. Do you want to live in a world of peace? See it and feel it, and creation is underway. Do you want to invent a new medical device? Ask for a download of information from Spirit to get you started and guide you as you go. When you align your higher mind with the abundance of your Source, nothing is out of reach. So spend time daydreaming daily and see where your mind will take you.

Move your awareness to your higher mind and feel the infinite love flowing through it. Intentionally extend that love to anyone and everyone for whom you may hold a grudge (and that includes you). Feel any anger or hurt softening and melting in the presence of your love.

Unplug from limiting beliefs in the world. On a piece of paper, list as many myths—messages that limit who you are and what's possible—as you can. For instance:

- Women over forty have as much chance of getting married as they have of being struck by lightning.

- You're too old to go back to school.

- If you don't have a nest egg by the time you're fifty, you'll never be able to retire.

- Soccer moms can't be sexy.

- Bad things come in threes.

You get the idea. We absorb these messages from the world around us. After you've listed as many myths as you can, cross out each one and replace it with a statement of what's true for *you*.

Spend twenty minutes each morning getting to a place of right-mindedness before you leave the house. Use prayer, meditation, and gratitude to help you remember the light that you are. Those twenty minutes will be an excellent investment in your day, saving you immeasurable time by freeing up your mental energy and allowing you to be guided by Spirit instead of the ego's resistance.

Look for the gift in everything. Know that there is no problem—no matter how complex or long-standing—that can't be solved by tuning into your light and asking for circumstances to be rearranged for the good of all.

Ask yourself how much time you spend time complaining—silently or aloud—about your boss, spouse, kids, or lawmakers. How much of your day is spent playing old tapes in your mind about your failures or regrets? How often do you miss what's going on in front of you because you're fretting about the future? Once you become aware of your fear-based thinking, ask yourself: How could I use that time and energy instead? What could I create if I used it in conjunction with my higher mind's infinite possibilities?

Before you enter into any situation or relationship, ask what the purpose is. As *A Course in Miracles* asks, "What is it for?" (Hint: Two excellent answers are "love" and "the highest good.") For instance, if you're going to talk to your partner about helping more around the house, you could use the conversation to complain and blame. Or you could use it for greater understanding and a deeper sense of partnership—not to mention a cleaner bathroom. Simply asking the question reminds you of who and what you are, attracts light into the situation, and sets up circumstances in which everyone wins.

Let's look at some examples of how you'll do things differently as you live your life in right-mindedness.

1. You grew up with parents who didn't have much good to say about the world. A part of you knew you could do great things, but there was never enough money for music lessons or sports, and your parents discouraged you from dreaming of a different life.

"The world is stacked against us," they said. "Good things happen to other people."

Even though you never quite bought in, their words have limited you, as though keeping yourself small is a way of respecting their beliefs. But now that you know you're the light and your mind has unlimited power, you realize that it serves no one to follow those old false beliefs.

So you close your eyes and focus on your connection to Spirit. This aligns you with your higher mind and unlimited possibilities. You give yourself permission to write down your goals and dreams, no matter how outlandish they seem. You review the list and ask for spiritual guidance in choosing the ones that will light you up. Then you set a goal of reaching out to someone each week who can give you information or support in accomplishing those goals.

When you get discouraged and the old ways start to call you back, remind yourself that you're the light of the world. As the light, you deserve joy, success, abundance, and peace, and you take another step forward toward your dreams.

2. Your husband needs to settle a bill with a customer who hasn't paid him yet. You need that money to pay your own bills. Meanwhile, your husband isn't sleeping well, and you suspect he's tossing and turning because he's anxious about a potential conflict with his customer.

Your ego mind is getting frustrated and impatient. It wants to say to your husband, "What are you waiting for? Don't be such a wimp. Get off your butt and go collect the money. I never would have married you if I knew you were going to be like this."

Clearly, this is not a proper use of the mind. You can't slam someone and feel good about yourself. Diminishing another's light always diminishes your own. And while it can incite action in the moment, it typically breeds resentment long-term.

Here's what you and your higher mind could say to your husband instead: "I know you don't like conflict. You want everyone to be happy—your client *and* us. And you want to be fair, sometimes so much so that you're unfair to yourself. I know that until you get this bill resolved, it's going to be eating at you, and I think that's where your sleep issue is coming from. The sooner you can deal with this, the better you'll feel. I trust you. I know you'll handle it well."

What does this do? It gives you a clear and compassionate voice, it restores the remembrance of light in both of you, and it frees your husband to resolve the situation from love instead of fear.

3. **A middle-school teacher watches one of her students walk into the classroom a few minutes late.** Before the student gets to her seat, she draws as much attention to herself as possible—drops a book on purpose, bumps into another student's chair, and hums to herself. She's calling for love from her ego mind—

the part of her that is always engaged in a push-pull of "I think I'm worthless, but I want people to see me."

Instead of the teacher reprimanding her in front of the class or sending her to detention, she starts the class, walks over to the student, and, without drawing attention from the rest of the group, quietly says to the student, "It's time to calm down now. I'm glad you're here."

Whoa. That's not what the student expected. A quiet voice. A welcome. A gentle directive. Affirmation. The teacher's message reminds the student that, underneath her defiance and bravado, she is the light.

That's the proper use of the mind.

⟶

Using your higher mind is not just about making more money or having more harmonious relationships. It's the difference between a peaceful world and one that blows itself up. If you're blowing up your life every day by attacking yourself or others with your thoughts, you're contributing to more chaos—even violence—in the world. But every time you think with your higher mind, you contribute to greater peace now and in the future.

It's important to remember that emotions result from thoughts. As *A Course in Miracles* says, "What is perceived as negative emotion is not the absence of love, but merely reversals of thought which are undermining love's power and goodness."

This is an essential point because your thoughts are the precursors to all your words, actions, and emotions—in other words, your entire human experience. If you struggle with shame, for instance, you may try counseling, coaching, and therapy. You may change your self-talk. You may develop new habits. But if you're taking all these steps with the same fear-based mind that created the shame in the first place, you have two choices: stuff it or try to change it. Either way, improvements will elude you or be temporary at best.

There's only one way to truly heal the guilt, shame, and other forms of ego fear: ask Spirit to heal your fear-based thoughts and restore your memory of the light that you are—a light in which fear in any form cannot exist.

Any time we allow ourselves or others to use our minds for negativity, self-pity, griping, gossip, hatred, or other forms of fear, we're teaching ourselves that we're *not* the light of the world. We're literally telling ourselves a lie. We're letting other people diminish themselves, and we're doing the same.

That's why becoming vigilant about how you use your mind—and which mind you're using—not only benefits you, but also changes how you interact with others and how they see themselves as well. The same fear that creates tension at home creates tension in communities and in the world. Much of our stress, overwhelm, and toxicity occurs because we hang out in the wrong mind—or what a client and I refer to as a "bad neighborhood"—and don't know there's an alternative. You don't need to fix, lament, or control the world. Instead, train yourself to think with the mind of love.

⁓

As you use your higher mind, what are some things you might think and say?

"Sometimes I get locked into seeing things a certain way or doing things just because I've always done them that way. But now I open up to considering new possibilities."

"I know I'm the light of the world, and because of that, I commit to using my mind for a higher purpose."

"I'm doing this because . . ." Then ask your higher Self and Spirit for the answer. Take time to consider the thoughts behind your actions, what your purpose is, what you want to accomplish. This is different from setting goals. This is higher-mind motivation.

What will change as you use your higher mind more consistently?

- ❀ You'll have more energy because you'll let go of the need for control.

- ❀ Old patterns of negativity, worthlessness, and hopelessness will be replaced by a brighter perspective, a sense of value, and possibilities.

- ❀ You'll feel more appreciative and grateful.

- ❀ You'll notice fewer conflicts in your life.

- ❀ You'll feel more confident about your actions.

- ❀ You'll be less reactive to life events, and they won't dominate your feelings.

- ❀ You'll be better able to trust yourself, other people, and Spirit.

❀ You'll honor the thoughts, words, and actions that flow through you from love.

⁓

It's important to remember that mastery of your mind is a lifelong journey. As you start using your higher mind more, you'll experience more of what you want in life and less of what you don't want. But you'll never eradicate the ego mind, so that needn't be your goal. In fact, if you try to escape or do away with your smaller mind, you'll simply amplify its effects by focusing on it.

The point is, we have ego minds in these human bodies, and we will always be affected by them some of the time. But you can shift from unconsciously being "victimized" by your fear-based thoughts to consciously choosing higher thoughts that serve you and the world. In other words, don't be discouraged by any lapses into fear. Simply use those times as a learning opportunity to choose love the next time around.

Remember: When you think and act from a higher mind, you're aided by limitless resources and support. When you think with the small mind, you trap yourself inside a compound of your own making. You get to choose which mind you think with, which one you listen to.

It's practical to use your higher mind. It saves time and effort. And it gets better results. So why wouldn't you use your mind for the greatest good possible? Why would you use it to stay stuck and sullen when you could use it to be expansive and joyful?

It's totally up to you. No matter the circumstances in your life, what situation you were born into, or what limitations you seem to bump up against every day, your mind will set your free if you let it. And when you know you're the light of the world, there's no question that you deserve to be free.

When you combine that freedom with Self-love, you'll be amazed at how your life will change. Which brings us, of course, to the next principle.

three

Foster Self-Love

When you know you're the light of the world and you use your powerful mind for the highest good, you're well on your way to living with Self-love. What's the love we're talking about? Not romantic love. Not a conditional love. Not a love that's based on getting or approving.

This is the divine love from which we were created, expressed from one light to another.

If we rely solely on our ego mind, we won't find the fulfillment, satisfaction, and joy that we seek. We'll always be engaged in frustration, depression, dissatisfaction, and anger. I'm capitalizing the *S* in Self-love because it recognizes the light that we are through our higher mind, with the help of Spirit.

You cannot hate yourself and love others. It's not possible. So the first step in loving the world—and bringing it peace—has to be in loving yourself. There is no other way.

We often think of Self-love as spending a day at the spa, indulging in a mani-pedi, and eating a kale salad. But that's just an attempt to take a break from the chaos in our fear-based minds.

The definition of Self-love is different. It means taking care of your Self by 1) consistently and intentionally living from your higher mind, and 2) trusting that, in conjunction with Source, you're expressing your light to create the highest and best for all. That's why it's so important to know you're the light and how powerful your higher mind is.

Self-love means talking to Source over and over again to remember and use your unique gifts and graces. As you do, you recognize your Self. Without this, you can intellectually know you're the light but still live in the darkness. You can know you have a higher mind but stubbornly ignore it. But when you foster Self-love, you intentionally choose your inner light and higher mind for your good and the good of others.

Let's take a look at essential elements of Self-love.

Self-love means trusting that Source knew what It was doing in creating you. Rather than looking to other people for cues about how to be acceptable, you come face to face with your best Self and say, "Hey, I know you! You've got that incredible gift for listening." Or bringing out the best in children. Or playing the clarinet. Or cleaning out closets. In other words, you honor your unique expression of love and light on this planet, no matter what anyone else thinks. You stand in the grandeur of who you are, knowing you don't need to apologize or ask permission.

It's important to note that there's no fear or anger in this. You're not isolating yourself and saying, "Screw everyone. I'm going to do it my way." Instead, you're simply being your Self with nothing to prove. "I'm going to be who I am, and I hope everyone else will, too."

Self-love comes from your commitment to use your mind for the highest good, which will bring you into right alignment with yourself and remind you that Self-love is your natural state. Everything outside you will continue to change, but the light that you are will not. This allows you to trust in:

- ❁ Divine timing.

- ❁ A bigger picture you can't see.

- ❁ Everything working for your good.

- ❁ The truth that God wants you to be happy.

- ❁ Your own Self-worth.

It's essential to build Self-love because the relationship you have with your Self and God will shape all your other relationships and interactions.

This runs much deeper than simply being in a decent mood or feeling good about yourself. Without Self-love, you're always subject to self-doubt, beating yourself up, comparing, and focusing on your mistakes instead of your strengths. And that's like constantly bobbing around on stormy waters, being buffeted by the winds. No wonder you feel exhausted and overwhelmed.

But when you live from Self-love, your foundation is solid. It doesn't matter what the rest of the world does, says, or thinks of you. You can trust the light that you are.

~

Imagine that a three-year-old says to you, "I'm bad. I don't deserve to be loved." How would you respond? Without hesitation, you would scoop up that three-year-old in your arms and say, "Of *course* you deserve to be loved. Don't ever let anyone tell you otherwise!"

You would have no doubt about this. Despite any misbehavior on the child's part, you'd have pure conviction and clarity when stating the obvious: Of course you deserve to be loved!

Your ego is like that three-year-old.

It has taken on messages, programming, and self-talk that say it's bad and not worthy of joy, peace, love, success, abundance, or well-being. But that's not true.

So here's what I want you to do: Start reacting to your own ego just the way you would to that three-year-old.

- ❀ When you hear your ego voice saying, "I'm not worthy," say instead, "Of course I'm worthy."

- ❀ When your ego voice says, "I'll never lose weight," say instead, "Of course I'll lose weight."

- ❀ When your ego voice says, "I don't deserve to do work I enjoy," say instead, "Of course I deserve to do work I enjoy."

- ❀ When your ego voice says, "I don't have anyone I can count on," say instead, "Of course I have people I can count on."

This does two things: It shows you how preposterous the ego's claims are, and it affirms that there's no need to live according to the ego's limited view of who you are—not when you're the light of the world.

~

Loving your Self means deciding what's going to have power over you and what's not. This comes down to what you value. If you value wrongly, *A Course in Miracles* says you won't have peace. Value rightly, and joy is yours.

This means you have to make a choice about what you want to rule your life. Will it be anger? Blame? Overwhelm? Illness? Scarcity? Poverty? Oppression? Despair? Or will it be hopefulness? Forgiveness? Acceptance? Gratitude? Prosperity? Abundance? Faith?

For instance, is your anger toward politicians going to rule you? Or are you going to respond to their actions by expressing your light? When your kids leave their dirty dishes in the sink, are you going to react with snarkiness or find a peaceful resolution? If a coworker tries to sabotage you, are you going to retaliate or have an honest conversation?

"Loving your
Self means deciding
what's going to have
power over you and
what's not."

Love your Self enough to value rightly, because what you choose as your overriding ideals will determine the quality of your life. You can be in what seem to be life's lowest circumstances. But if you climb onto a higher ideal, you can soar.

The most powerful and Self-loving thing you can do is decide who and what you are and what's right for you, then claim it. Once you do that, you're invulnerable to other people's judgments and opinions.

So what can you do to foster Self-love?

Build trust by talking to Spirit every morning and night. In addition, say thank you for spiritual guidance at least a dozen times throughout the day. Develop your relationship with Spirit so it becomes as tangible a source of support as your friends and family.

Surround yourself with joy. Place at least one message of joy—a plaque, a river rock, a poster, a refrigerator magnet—in every room of your house. Create an environment that reminds you what you are.

Get honest with yourself. Ask yourself questions that will give you clarity: Am I doing this to win people's approval? Or because it's what I want and believe? Is this an expression of my light? Or am I going along with what the world says, even though it doesn't serve me? As you ask and receive answers, you'll build a relationship with your Self, becoming better acquainted with the light that you are and how to express it.

Practice using and sharing your unique gifts. If you love to paint, do more of it and sell your creations or give them away. If you're adept at fixing things, find others who want to learn and teach them. If you're great at organizing things, help a friend clean out her kitchen cupboards. As you express your gifts in the world, you'll be blessed by the sharing, which will strengthen your sense of Self.

Prepare more meals with love, and bless everything you eat. These simple actions literally nourish you with light, energizing your Self and your connection with others.

Apologize when you've spilled your fear all over someone. This will wipe the slate clean for both of you so you're not carrying any guilt, anger, or regret.

Identify a situation in your life that has been stewing or left unattended for a while. It could be a conversation you need to have, a bill you need to pay, or an argument you need to resolve. Leaving things unattended saps your energy and indicates a lack of trust and Self worth. So remember the light that you are, ask Spirit for help, and allow your Self to be led to a resolution. When you bring love to the situation, you can take care of it more easily than you might think.

Remember that you're always talking to yourself. Any time you express thoughts, words, or actions that are meant to hurt others, you're always hurting yourself. There are no exceptions. That's why the Golden Rule isn't just a moral commandment, it's also good mental health. If you call someone an idiot in your mind or aloud, you're disrespecting yourself. If you watch TV and think to yourself, "Wow, she's ugly," you're talking to yourself. If you condemn the driver who just cut in front of you, you're punishing yourself. Because these fear-based attacks— spoken and unspoken—are so ubiquitous, they literally make us sick individually and collectively. But we can cure the dis-ease by thinking and speaking from the light instead, which is the ultimate act of Self-love.

What does Self-love in action look like? Here are a few examples.

1. Your brother is trying to create a family reunion invitation but doesn't know how to use the online software. He's frustrated and comes to you saying, "I'm not getting a god-damned thing done" and asks for your help.

Without knowing that both of you are the light of the world, you might throw his anger back in his face and bark at him as you fix the document, then call him an idiot under your breath. "Why does he always have to be such a jerk? He's been this way our whole lives. Why did I get stuck with a brother like this?" This inner dialogue can easily ruin your day. You have to ask, "Why would I do that to my Self? Do I really want to trade my peace for *that?*"

When you practice Self-love, you know that everything you do for your brother, you're doing for yourself. Your inner dialogue might change to something like this: "I get it. His fear and frustration are talking. He's afraid of being seen as a goof-up again. I don't have to make his whole life wrong. I can either respond from fear or from truly wanting to help.

Which one is going to help both of us remember who and what we are? Which one will feel better to me in the end?"

Remember: Every time we see others as the light, we remind ourselves of what we are, too.

And if you forget that you're the light of the world and don't respond with peace? No worries. Say, "I'm sorry" and move on. You'll have another chance before you know it.

2. You're deeply concerned about the issue of immigration, and you feel called to join a protest march coming up in a couple of weeks. Every time you think about it, you can feel your ego rising up with anger, indignation, and despair. You want to make your voice heard and stand up for what you believe, but you wonder if the energy of the crowd will make you feel worse instead of better.

As a practice of Self-love, you spend time reflecting on why and how you want to be part of the march, and you realize that you want to be present with love. You want to stand in the crowd as the light that you are and bring that energy and intention to the gathering.

Maybe you make a sign or wear a T-shirt that says what you're for rather than what you're against. Maybe you ask

Spirit to be with you and everyone in the march so you can foster understanding and conciliation. Maybe you set an intention to march with respect for all—even those with different views.

When you bring that kind of energy to any gathering—whether it's you and one other or you and thousands—you can trust that it makes a difference, because you're expressing higher energy and extending light to all.

3. You feel like you're stuck in a rut. Your kids have grown up, your husband's busy with work, and when you wake up in the morning, the only thing you look forward to is going back to sleep that night.

You realize you're bored with life, and you don't know what to do about it because you spent the last twenty-five years taking care of everyone else. When you ask yourself, "What would make me excited about life again?" you draw a blank.

A vacation? You hate to spend the money. A volunteer project? It's hard to imagine you'd have the energy. A cooking class? You've already prepared enough meals for a lifetime.

Clearly, those responses come from the ego, which will find a reason to redirect any avenue toward joy. And so, instead of looking for answers in the external world, you go inside and get reacquainted with the light that you are.

You ask yourself, "When was I happiest and most enthused about my life?"

Then you pose this question: "What did I know about myself then that I have since forgotten?"

Dig into that answer, and you're likely to strike gold. Because in some way, somehow, it will lead you back to the light that you are.

—✦—

Here are a few other things to know about Self-love.

- ❀ The way you respond to others will tell you a lot about your own light and Self-love. If a guarded person causes you to shut down, you've got your own blockages to look at. If a guarded person prompts you to send blessings to them while you stay in a place of peace, then your light is shining freely.

- ❀ Because you're always talking to yourself, listening to what you say—or want to say—to others will be a good benchmark of your own Self-love.

❧ If you're always seeking approval or love from the external world without feeling it in yourself, you'll spend your life wandering, looking for permission to be who you are, searching for external validation of your right to exist. One minute your partner sends you flowers and you feel loved. The next minute someone elbows past you on the subway and you feel invisible. This is why we see the world as an ugly and dangerous place: because we're hoping to trust it with our Self-worth, and it continually disappoints us. But your Self-worth is not "out there." It is in you and your connection to Source. Whenever you start looking for it in a relationship or a possession or a belief or an institution, you're setting up a love-hate relationship with the world and yourself.

❧ Remember that the light is in you. Look inside. Look inside. Look inside. Don't be afraid. Your ego will post guards at the door and try to convince you not to go in, but there is nothing but light inside you.

❁ When you're certain of your light, you can live your life with passion and purpose, and without fear of being taken advantage of. Knowing and loving yourself doesn't just mean knowing your preferences, your strengths and weaknesses, your idiosyncrasies, your gifts. It means knowing what you are as well as who you are. When you're confident in that, you will have passion for life and your contributions to it.

❁ Self-love allows you to let go of grievances. The fact is, grievances are nothing more than your own ego fears looking for someone to blame.

Here's a simple example: My husband unloads the dishwasher. Sometimes. When he doesn't do it, my ego gets huffy. "What? Does he think his life is busier than mine? He watched football all night. How come he's not doing his share around here?"

Now, if I'm honest, he did do the laundry, mow the yard, and pay the bills. But my ego always wants to win—even if it means fudging the score. So, if I allow my ego to hold onto its grievance, I'm choosing frustration over Self-love. I am actively dimming my light. That's why, when you realize that holding a grudge isn't nearly as important as being happy, Self-love is yours.

❀ When you foster Self-love, you have no need to be jealous of other people's wealth, good fortune, or happy relationships because you know that you have success, abundance, and love within you. As you practice the principle of Self-love, you'll shed anything that's blocking those natural qualities so you can manifest money, health, and harmony in your life, too.

What are the signs that you're practicing Self-love?

❀ You feel solid. Not rigid, but clear. You know what you are and what you believe.

❀ You meet your own needs as well as the needs of others.

- You no longer invest in the idea of stress or struggle. You trust that life can be easier and simpler without giving up anything you value.

- You have a sense of purpose because you know you're the light.

- You no longer feel like you're working around someone else's moods or demands.

- You trust that all things are working on your behalf.

- You're clear about what you want and what you don't want, and you set appropriate boundaries.

- When you ask Spirit for something in your life, you use this phrase: "This, please, or something better."

- You are unflappable, carrying a posture of peace and possibility into the world.

- You actively look for simple ways to extend kindness to strangers every day, such as writing a note of thanks to your waiter at the bottom of the credit card bill or complimenting a convenience store clerk on her hair. By doing this, you turn ordinary interactions into opportunities to make someone's day, thereby creating a more peaceful world.

❧ Instead of meeting attack with attack, you send love to bullies—no matter how infamous they may be— because you know they're simply acting out of fear.

❧ You're generous because you know your needs are met, and the more love you share, the more you'll have.

❧ You feel free to speak and act without fear of judgment because you're unaffected by other people's opinions of you.

❧ You know it's not selfish to say what you want, and it's not weak to ask for help.

⟿

Self-love is about you and God. Not about you and your pastor, you and your teacher, you and your guru, you and the people who govern your country. It is an inner knowing and light.

That's why everything in this book always comes back to you. If you want to find ways to bring peace to a chaotic world, to bring more harmony to your family, to uplift and inspire your community, look inside your Self and ask Spirit. Ask the light that you are.

As you do this, you'll be equipped to see only love, which brings us to our next principle.

four

See Only Love

You know you're the light of the world. You're committed to using your higher mind for the good of all. You foster the Self-love that comes from trust in a higher power. Because of that, you're now able to shift your vision and see only love.

If this seems like something a superhero might do, you're right. It is, indeed, a superpower, because it gives you the ability to see what others can't, right injustices, and restore peace in a chaotic world. And, it is completely available to you right now.

Why is seeing only love important in being the light of the world? Because it keeps you focused on what's real. It reminds you who and what you are. It helps you handle personal situations and world events without getting overwhelmed.

It also makes it possible to find the gifts in situations that seem "wrong." For instance, maybe you've been tired and headachy for a couple of weeks. Your ego sees this as a sign of illness. But what if you saw it differently? What if your body simply needed extra rest to catch up with your soul growth?

Or maybe your parents ignored your musical gifts when you were a child, convincing you to take business courses instead. Now, as an adult, your ego could blame your family for trying to make you someone you weren't (and you could beat yourself up for allowing it). Or you could see only love in the situation and realize the gifts you were born with are still there. Plus, your parents thought they were doing right by you, even though they were letting their own fears about your well-being get in their way.

This is what happens when you have new vision. You don't pretend or stick your head in the sand, but you see a new interpretation of events—one in which everything and everyone is working for your highest good. If you're looking through the lens of love rather than the lens of fear, it makes sense that you're going to see with more compassion, less blame, more understanding, and less anger.

The teachers we honor, from Jesus to Martin Luther King Jr., saw beyond fear to love because they weren't looking through the lens of the ego. And that's the key.

Seeing only love is not about *what* you see. It's about the eyes you see *through*.

What does it mean to see only love? It means you no longer want to diminish yourself or anyone else. Instead you affirm and build consensus. You see people who disagree with you as the light that they are rather than your enemy. In fact, they may be your greatest teachers.

This shift in vision is a natural extension of Self-love. But be aware that you may experience pushback from the fear-based voices around you. If you see beauty rather than ugliness, you're accused of ignoring reality. If you choose to watch positive news or avoid the news altogether, you're a Pollyanna. "Get real," the world says. In other words, "Who do you think you are? Come be miserable like us."

The ego, in fact, wants to be part of the world's soap opera, in which characters come and go, but the plot never really changes. If you retreated to a cabin in the woods without access to the news and reentered the world a year later, you'd see the power of the ego's status quo. War? Still raging. Political squabbles? Still front and center. Poverty and famine? Still unresolved.

No wonder it seems hard to see only love. With all that fear-based noise around us, we have no idea how beautiful this world is.

"*Looking through the lens of love means you will see with more compassion, less blame, and less anger.*"

But seeing only love actually isn't difficult at all. The only thing that stops us is the ego's insistence on staying stuck. It's effortless to change the focus of your thoughts, shifting your vision from hardships and struggles to the beauty in and around you. In fact, you can do it right now, wherever you are, no matter what's going on in your world.

Rather than lamenting the money you don't have, think of the money you do. Instead of replaying a slight or insult in your mind, remember a gesture of kindness. Instead of focusing on disagreements within our world, honor the freedom we have to disagree.

In this very moment, you can focus on something you love in your partner or child. Celebrate the immense resilience of humanity. Give thanks to the person who made the chair you're sitting in or who built the house or apartment that gives you shelter and warmth.

This is a simple, economical, and effective way to change your life, your health, your finances, and your relationships. Why? Because everything you want to improve will shift automatically just by seeing love rather than fear.

Here are a few essential points about seeing only love.

Years ago in *A Course in Miracles* class, my co-teacher and I made some flash cards. Each one showed a recognizable figure or character, such as Santa Claus, Jesus, Julia Child, a baby—people you have warm and fuzzy feelings about. But we also made other flash cards showing a terrorist, Hitler, and Freddy Krueger.

In the class, we presented the flashcards one by one, starting with the warm and fuzzies. We asked the class, "Can you love this person?" As they saw Santa, of course the answer was yes. A baby? No question. Julia Child? Who couldn't love Julia Child?

Then we got to a terrorist wearing a hood and carrying an assault rifle. "Can you love this person?" Hesitation. We could feel everyone's discomfort as they wrestled with the fear the images prompted in their ego minds. Some people mumbled, "Well, kind of . . . maybe . . ." Others simply shook their heads and said a resolute no. We got the same response to Hitler. Same with Freddy Krueger.

Their response reflected the inner turmoil we experience in the world every day when faced with people and situations we've been taught are "wrong." But here's the thing. We weren't asking, "Can your fear-based ego love another person's fear-based ego?" We also weren't asking, "Can you condone their fear-based actions?"

Instead, we were asking, "Can the light in you see past the fear to love the light within that other person, even when he's the most heinous criminal on the planet? Can you love the truth in him, no matter how disguised it may be with violence and depravity? Are you willing to let your high Self see and acknowledge his high Self?"

In other words, we weren't looking at sin or brokenness or evil. We were looking at love. The kind of love that's not defined or limited by the package in which it resides.

This flashcard exercise elicited an extreme reaction because the figures we showed are extreme symbols. But the questions about love and light are the same, whether you're encountering a stranger on the subway or your neighbor down the street. Are you willing to let your light see the light in others?

So what if my definition of love looks different than your definition of love? Ah. Now things really get interesting.

One person may love going to the gym, whereas another despises it. One person thinks hunting is uncivilized, another

80

sees it as a way to honor the cycles of nature. Our choices are not innately good or bad. What varies is the meaning we give them.

For example, let's look at one of the most controversial issues in this world: ending another person's life. As a society, we've set up what may seem like logical rules for when the human race can kill people and when we can't. Killing someone on the battlefield is honorable. A robber killing someone during a break-in is punishable by law.

Killing a criminal by electrocution is accepted by some. Killing a child in school sparks a national movement for change. The issue of abortion has caused some protesters to kill adults out of anger about killing fetuses.

Now, we're not talking about a complicated edict here. "Thou shalt not kill" is about as clear as it gets. Yet we still find ways to justify and defend the meaning we give it.

Killing a person is killing a person. The end result is the same. It's the meaning we give to it that varies. (And, by the way, even if we don't physically kill someone, we may murder them with thoughts of attack and anger.)

Our egos manipulate meaning to suit our purposes and make us feel less afraid or guilty. Life seems so complicated because our egos are constantly making meaning and proclaiming "right" and "wrong." Are cloth napkins better than paper? Does one religion have all the answers? Is one investment advisor more reliable than another?

In contrast, your higher mind has only one meaning for everything: love.

Trying to defend your meaning and make another person wrong will not be effective. But bringing love into the equation with shared intention will. This is what we call "common ground," the place at which we can begin to move forward—together, and in the light.

When you see only love, you're constantly reminding yourself of who you are. You're recognizing yourself as a loving and compassionate being.

Having said this, it's important to remember that people are always working within their current level of understanding and perceptions. To a person who believes a whole-house alarm system is essential for a family's safety, putting an alarm system on their house is an act of love.

To a person who believes alarm systems aren't necessary because trust will do a better job, the person who puts up an alarm is throwing their money away.

Seeing only love does not mean pretending everything is okay when it's not. It means actively choosing to see the light rather than the darkness, using the sight that comes from your higher mind and your own illumination.

⌒

Seeing only love is easy to say, right? But how do you do this and do it consistently?

Ask for your fear-based thoughts about seeing only love to be healed, because your ego will not believe in or support this way of living. Start with a willingness to see only love, then continue to ask for your ego fears to be healed so your path will be clear.

Next, develop different habits, just as you would if you started flossing daily or paid all your bills on the first of the month. Seeing only love is a habit you can develop with the help of Spirit who, if you ask, will heal the resistance you'll feel from your fear-based mind.

How do you make a habit of it? Start each morning as soon as you wake up. Say thank you to Spirit, your Self, and all your relationships. Focus on three things you're grateful for that represent beauty and love to you. Recognize that everything carries the meaning you give it, so resolve to give the external world the meaning of love rather than fear.

Shift your vision to see with your higher mind rather than the ego mind. This means looking at any situation and asking, "Where is the love here?" What are the gifts? What is the lesson? How can I respond with compassion rather than anger?

For instance, if you look at a tree from your ego mind, you may see the sticks you have to pick up after every storm and the leaves you'll have to rake in the fall. If you see it with the mind of love, you'll see the shade it provides, the fragrance of the flowers in the spring, and the beauty it brings to the landscape.

The tree hasn't changed. What changed is the mind you think with, the eyes you see with. Which one is going to make you feel more peaceful? Which will bring you more joy?

Start each day by asking to be used for the highest good. Ask Spirit to put you where you're needed and give you words that will help your Self and others. Let go of when and how these opportunities might occur, then be willing to act when you feel the nudge.

For instance, a woman I know stepped into a potential brawl because she felt compelled to intervene, interrupting fear with love. It happened when an intoxicated young man accidentally knocked over another person's beer at a party, and he was about to get punched for it. When she saw what was happening, she didn't let her own fears stop her. Instead, she walked into the middle of the situation with a voice of calm and caring. Within a couple of minutes, she found the young man a ride home, bought the aggressor a beer, and stilled a potentially violent situation. What gave her the confidence and protection to do it? Her ability to see only love in the moment.

Yes, your ego will say she was foolish. But remember that you have a spiritual presence as well as a physical one. Never underestimate what's possible when you combine your higher vision with a willingness to be used for the highest good.

What does it look like to see only love? Here are a few situations that illustrate the power of shifting your vision.

1. You messed up. At least your ego thinks so, and it's not letting you forget about it. You wrote an email with rude comments about a coworker and accidentally sent it to the wrong email address. It ended up in the hands of . . . that coworker.

Obviously you weren't seeing only love or you wouldn't have written the email in the first place, but that's in the past. Your ego will want to take you back there and pummel you. But shift to your higher mind instead so you can focus on what seeing only love looks like now.

First, it means getting honest with yourself about why you wrote the message and what that person was triggering in you, because you were talking to yourself when you wrote it. Then tap into your greatest strength—your vulnerability— and make amends. You might say something like, "I want to apologize for what I wrote. The things I said were rude, and, more important, they weren't true. I hope you'll forgive me."

This will strengthen the light in you, so the experience will serve a purpose. You'll actually expand your love. How your coworker responds, of course, is up to her, but you could ask

Spirit to use the situation for healing so you both can look at it with love.

2. You're out with friends, all of whom have similar political views. The conversation turns to complaints about the current elected officials, and the energy starts to build. Your friends are not arguing with each other because they're all in agreement. Instead, they're piling on, and what starts with dissatisfaction turns to all-out fury and indignation about decisions coming out of Washington and the people in charge.

You've been here before and know this conversation could go on for hours, ramping up with more attacks. You know that the time and energy could be spent a different way, and so you float a suggestion to the group: "So here's a question I've been thinking about lately," you say, "and I want to know what you guys think. What if we envisioned the leaders we'd like to have in office? What would they be like? Tell me about your ideal leader."

This changes the conversation and redirects the energy. In doing so, it focuses on creating something new rather than reinforcing what no longer serves you. You do this because you know that if we took the energy we spend on complaining about how things are and used it for envisioning what we'd like it to be, we could manifest anything. Staying focused on what's not working just gets us more of what's not working.

As the conversation with your friends develops, it may drift back into griping. "Yeah, I'd like to see people with integrity . . . something those bums in Washington wouldn't recognize if you served it to 'em on a plate."

Instead of letting the conversation revert to venting, you ask another question. "Integrity. That's such a good word. What does it mean to you?" In other words, get people talking in a forward direction rather than going backward.

Asking "What if" questions is an easy way to redirect energy without looking naïve or having people dismiss you for having your head in the sand. It takes the focus off of you and gives others the opportunity to think about their own beliefs differently. Still, there's likely to be at least one person who will say, "Why are we talking about what we want? Things are never going to change. They've always been a mess. That's just how life is."

No need to argue or try to talk them out of it. This is probably something they've heard others say or they've said a thousand times before. It's the perfect time to see only love by affirming the light in them: "Yeah, things can seem messed up sometimes, but I've seen you make things better in all sorts of ways. You're a terrific parent, you're always the first one there to help a friend, and you've inspired me more times than I can count. You may not realize it, but you are making the world better, and I for one want to say thank you."

Did you notice? The light just got a little brighter.

3. **You look at wars raging around the world and think, "How could I possibly see the love in this?"** Go within, speak to Spirit, and say, "I don't know why this is happening, but I know you do. I want to see this as a call for love so I can be part of healing it. Please extend love through me to parts of the world that need it. I trust that you'll use it for the highest good."

Use your visualization skills to see the world flooded with peace and light and love. Pour love into places of conflict like North Korea and Syria. See the Earth swaddled in a blanket of love.

Know this is real. You have engaged the light of your superpower, and it will not be wasted.

Seeing only love may feel impossible, but here's an easy way to wrap your mind around it: I was talking with one of my *A Course in Miracles* students about love and fear. We call her the Course Whisperer because she has a gentle way of dropping *Miracles* teachings into conversations with her clients. For instance, when a mom complained that her children weren't becoming star soccer players, the Course Whisperer said, "Well, maybe you could just encourage them to be who they are instead."

See what I mean?

She calls her ego Igor. And one day she asked a great question. A very great question: What if she was in the middle of a good day, and Igor just never showed up?

Holy cow. An Igor-less day. An Igor-less world. Can you imagine?

Well, obviously, Igor can't imagine it and wouldn't want to try. But your higher Self won't hesitate. In fact, it knows that Igor never had any power to begin with. When you have an Igor-less day or moment, you'll see that love, and nothing but love, was there all along. Igor was just hiding it behind his cape and distracting you with his juggling.

That's the only story there is, no matter how many different ways it looks. When you not only are surrounded by love, but you're the embodiment of it, nothing but love can result. So why don't we make this an Igor-less day and see it right now? No fear, no judgment.

And that, of course, brings us to our next principle.

five

Meet Others
Without Judgment

Once you decide to see only love, you can relinquish judgment and see people for what they are. In the end, as with every principle in this book, everyone benefits, including you.

As it says in *A Course in Miracles*, "You have no idea of the tremendous release and deep peace that comes from meeting yourself and your brothers totally without judgment."

Ahhh . . . do you feel the peace in that?

So, what does it mean to meet others without judgment? First, let's look at the idea of oneness.

⌇

We often hear the word "oneness," along with phrases like, "There's only one of us here." But in a world with billions of birth certificates, Social Security numbers, and driver's licenses, how can we all be one?

Maybe it would help to think of it this way: Have you ever tried to separate air from itself?

Ever tried to grab a little oxygen and hold it in your hand? Or trap some O_2 inside a jar or in a balloon?

It always finds a way back to being part of the atmosphere, doesn't it?

No matter how you try to separate it from all the other air, it's still part of the same whole.

That's what love is like—the divine love that made us, and the love that we are.

Spiritual teachings are consistent in saying nothing can separate us from the love of God—or from one another—because we, like oxygen, are always a part of that love.

All of us. All in it together.

It's a hard concept to grasp because our human minds are so used to how things look, with their distinct shapes and forms. Your mother seems separate from your daughter. Your dog seems separate from the squirrel it chases. You and your sister appear to be distinct and, with an occasional disagreement, divided.

After all, everyone has a different body, a unique personality, an individual story.

But all of us are part of the same vast atmosphere of love. Inseparable, indefinable, unchangeable.

This is where we come to understand that everyone in our lives—especially those who challenge us and make us uncomfortable—are our master teachers, because they give us the opportunity to heal what's in us, not what's in them.

At this juncture, we realize there is no enemy, there is no other. And that includes God.

We realize that judgment of others is the same as judging ourselves, and vice versa.

And because we are all One, conflict between one and another can't exist except in the mind of the ego.

Which means that it doesn't really exist at all.

Here are some essential points about oneness and how it relates to judgment.

The belief in separation is the root of all fear. If we believe in divine love, we're called to live without judging ourselves or others and know that we are one.

We know we "shouldn't" judge, yet we do it without thinking, as automatically and unconsciously as breathing. We see a photo of someone and immediately make judgments based on the color of his hair. We see the condition of someone's car and make judgments about her character. We look at a tattoo or a burqa or the book someone's reading and make assumptions based on our own past experience, not on the light of the person standing right in front of us. In fact, if we're looking through the eyes of judgment, we don't really see that person at all. We simply see our own fears, insecurities, and expectations projected onto them and the world around us.

That's why, if we want to grow as spiritual beings but we're still judging ourselves and others, then we're negating the very nature of divine love itself. You can't have it both ways.

The world would change in an instant if we really got this. And your whole world *can* change in an instant when you start practicing this day by day.

⌒

Do you want to know one of the fastest ways to remember what you are? Send a little love to your "enemies." When you do that, you know the love is not coming from outside yourself, so it must be coming from you and Source energy. That means you *are* light. You *are* love.

The ego's version of "love your enemies" is: Do it even though they may trample you and take advantage of you. Take the higher road and love them anyway. But that's not it. Love your enemies so you will remember the love that *you* are.

Want an indivisible world? Become indivisible in yourself. Stop carving yourself up into little pieces through judgment, self-doubt, and fear. Accept and love all of who you are. No exceptions.

"When you relinquish judgment, you set aside all expectations. You let things –and especially people– be as they are."

Love your hair color. Love your weight. Love the decisions you've made, even the ones you'd do differently. Love your mistakes, your voice, your strength, what you consider your weaknesses. Love your successes and what you call your failures. Love it all. Then you will be indivisible. And think of what peace there is in that.

We see people as we want them to be. One person looks at a politician and sees a savior, an upstanding citizen, a reasonable man with good ideas, at least in part because he belongs to the "right" political party. Another person looks at the same politician and sees a crook and a manipulator who is only out for himself, at least in part because he's with the "wrong" party.

But this goes even deeper. We not only see people as a reflection of what we believe. *We make people into what we need them to be.*

For instance, a single mom makes her ex-husband into a deadbeat to reinforce her belief that she doesn't deserve support. She sees him as worthless, and he stops sending child support. "See?" she tells a friend. "It's not worth the time to try to get any money out of him. He hasn't lifted a finger for his daughter for the last three years." In other parts of his life, the ex-husband may make responsible decisions. But he plays the role his ex-wife assigned because it's what she expects him to be.

We shape others by what we see in them. In fact, our perceptions don't have anything to do with them at all. We simply create attributes that reinforce our own beliefs.

That's why a child who is a terror at home can be every teacher's favorite. It's why a sibling who is considered the black sheep in the family can be a role model to community youth.

As we've seen before, we bring meaning to everything in our lives. But when we do this from the hornet's nest of conflicting desires, we assign people roles based on our own ego needs. Only by relinquishing judgment can we erase the script for ourselves and others, allowing everyone to simply be the light that they are.

We can't judge because we don't have all the facts. Our ego minds judge others for their skin color, sexual orientation, what they wear, how they talk, and the choices they make. But we're not qualified to judge anyone or anything for one simple reason: We can't see the big picture.

A classic Zen story illustrates this point. Here's an updated version:

You come down with the flu. Bad. Because you're sick, you don't have to drive to work on icy roads. Good. Because you're not at work, you miss out on Employee Appreciation Day and a free lunch. Bad. Since you're not at the office, your coworkers make plans for your birthday celebration. Good.

You get the idea. Our ego mind is quick to pounce on anything it could label "bad," but that experience may be just what we need to deliver us to our greatest joy. As *A Course in Miracles* says, "Judgment is confused with wisdom and substitutes for truth." Our judgment is based on inconsistent criteria because everything simply has the meaning we give it.

In order to judge anything, we'd have to be—well, God—because only Spirit has all the information. And besides, there's nothing to judge anyway. How can you judge love and light?

When you relinquish judgment, you set aside all expectations. You let things—and especially people—be as they are. You toss the old baggage in the dumpster, and you meet everyone as though you're seeing them for the first time, even if you've known them your whole life. This allows you to stand in a neutral position—a position of light. You wipe the whole slate clean.

You read comments from a senator who supports the NRA. No judgment.

You read comments from a senator who condemns the NRA. No judgment.

You think through your own stand on the issue and feel confident about your choice. No judgment.

No cheering, no jeering, no heckling, no name-calling, no self-righteousness. Simply witnessing.

You apply the principle of oneness and remember we're all connected.

Because of that, you know that you're one with the senator on both sides of the aisle. Some of my *A Course in Miracles* students have great ways of reminding themselves of this daily. When they look at someone, they say, "You're afraid to be seen, and so am I." Or, "You attack others, and so do I." Or, "You have a big heart, and so do I." Or, "You are love and light, and so am I."

Okay, now let's take a leap and think of saying that about a school shooter.

I can hear the chorus of ego voices saying, "Are you crazy? I'm supposed to see light in someone who murdered children?"

Yes. Because the light is there. Granted, it's covered up with so much muck and fear that you have to shift to your higher mind, your spiritual eyes, to see it, but it's there.

It can't *not* be there because that person is a child of divine love just like you. The difference is that when you forget what you are, you snap at your husband or eat a quart of ice cream. When the shooter forgot what he was, he loaded a gun.

That's the hallmark of applying these principles. You understand that the two attacks, even though one seems much darker than the other, came from the same place of fear.

And both deserve compassion, forgiveness, and remembrance of the light.

~

How does your life change when you give up judgment and operate from an understanding of oneness?

* You become more honest because you were never capable of judging anyway. When you adopt a neutral

position, you allow a higher knowing to flow through you.

❖ You interrupt the knee-jerk reactions and prejudices you've picked up from the world, and you witness what's right in front of you rather than what you've been taught to see.

❖ You no longer feel the pain, struggle, and loneliness that come from judging yourself and others.

❖ You become more aware of the thoughts you send into the world, and you work with Spirit more intentionally to send messages that support rather than diminish.

❖ You stop wishing other people would change to make you happy.

❖ You stop hating the people who look and live differently than you do.

❖ You see social media as an external representation of our oneness, making you more likely to use it to build a better world rather than using it to judge or blame others and act from fear.

❀ You realize that our thoughts are all connected. They carry just as much energetic power as the more visible and audible parts of who we are. Because of this, you can't attack yourself and others in your mind, then go out and serve food at the homeless shelter and effectively spread peace. Do the inner work first, then carry it with you everywhere you go.

⟿

So how do you start the practice of relinquishing judgment? Here are a few steps to start.

Focus on this quote from *A Course in Miracles:* "Peace to my brother, who is one with me. Let all the world be blessed with peace through us." Take time to reflect on it, and say the words silently to everyone you meet throughout the day—especially to those who may pose some challenges in your life. This is an ideal way to shift to the truth about unity.

Sit in silence for ten minutes every day and focus on the thoughts, words, and actions of love going on around the world. Isn't it odd that we're perfectly ready to feel threatened by the ruler of North Korea, but we don't stop to think about the people of North Korea who are contributing love to this planet?

I can let myself be diminished by angry words from a talk show host—even if I never listen to the show. But I don't think about the millions of expressions of love going on around the world every single day.

We don't have to be present to hear those words or see those smiles for them to impact us. Because we're all one, we feel every angry word spoken by any ego anywhere. *And* we feel all the love.

Take in those expressions of love. Bring them into your heart. Receive their gifts. Feel how they remind you of the truth of who you are. Say thank you for them, expressing your gratitude to your brothers and sisters around the world.

As you sit, you might think about things like:

* Mothers singing their babies a lullabye.

* People saying, "I love you" before they hang up the phone.

- Teachers patting their students on the backs and saying, "Good job."

- Shopkeepers putting out an "Open" sign for the day and looking forward to greeting their customers.

- People helping someone across the street.

- Health professionals saving a person's life.

- Friends lending comfort.

- Laughter.

- Pots of soup to feed the hungry.

The list is endless, but you get the idea. Let your high Self and your inner guidance tune into all the good happening around the world. And give thanks, knowing your gratitude will help others remember who they are as part of divine love.

Pay attention to your language. Our words can imply unity or separation, acceptance or judgment. It's not hard to flip the switch from one to the other. We just need to be aware, find new words, and practice. Here are some examples:

"Why did you do *that?*" The question sounds like instant blame, and it's meant to make the person you're talking to feel ashamed and small, which means *you* feel ashamed and small.

Flip the switch to these words: "Help me understand . . ." This phrase can be said with respect. You're not assigning blame. You're not making the other person wrong. You're simply asking for more information. These words can encourage a conversation rather than stopping it in its tracks.

"It's your fault." This is the ego's valiant attempt to focus on what's wrong and then make another person pay for it.

Flip the switch to these words: "How can I help?" Instant unity. We're in this together. You're not offering to fix the problem, but you're saying, "I won't abandon you."

"*Now* what are you going to do?" More finger-pointing, with a thinly disguised connotation of "You're on your own."

Flip the switch to these words: "What do you need in this moment?" Those are words of solidarity. They imply, "Let's focus on a solution rather than the problem."

Follow the model of nonviolent activism. That movement teaches us to "Build relationship rather than victory." Spirit and the higher Self do exactly that, whereas the ego wants to win.

Winning, of course, can present itself in a lot of different ways—everything from making someone feel small or ashamed to having the last word.

But unity only presents itself one way: everyone involved feels honored and uplifted.

We can see unity even in competition. Good sportsmanship, for instance, means that the winning team may go home with the trophy, but they congratulate the other team for being honorable opponents.

When you view everyday situations as opportunities to build relationship rather than victory, you'll see them in a different light.

Think of a change you want to see in your household, workplace, or community. Hold that vision, detach from the need to win, and let your ability to see only love erase the differences and separations. If you are judging someone, visualize him standing in front of you and bless him with your light, then feel blessed by his.

And remember: Those who tear down others may exert false power for a while, but they can't stand for long. Fear is a temporary teacher, an insufficient substitute. For lasting change, only love will do.

Recognize that you can set boundaries and say no to the unacceptable without judging. Go inside first, become clear about what is and isn't right for you, and state your preferences and boundaries. You don't have to judge the other person or make them wrong. You're simply saying what you will and won't allow in your world.

Build unity by sending grateful energy through the Internet. Let's say you're reading a product review online, and one review in particular is helpful to you. Take a few moments to look at the name of the person who wrote it and send them love, knowing that Spirit will deliver it for you. Send them gratitude and blessings. It will remind you of who you are and send some needed love through the ethers. Look for other ways to make the Internet a highway of kindness and appreciation.

Pay attention to how quickly and automatically we view others' choices through our own preferences. You go shopping with a friend who tries on a dress and you think to yourself, "I would never wear that." Great. You're not the one trying it on. Or you go out to eat with your coworker and think, "You're putting ketchup on sushi?" Good news. You don't have to.

We judge others' choices out of our own preferences rather than respecting theirs. Everyone has a right to their preferences; your job is to be clear about what you want and ask for it out of Self-love.

⟪⟫

What does relinquishing judgment look like in everyday life? Here are a few illustrations.

I. **You're in the middle of a crowded place, like a movie theater or subway.** You look around at everyone and think to yourself, "I belong to everyone here, and they belong to me."

When your ego tries to make exceptions and says, "Well, everyone except that man with the dirty jeans who hasn't shaved in a couple of weeks," see the light in him. Truly, look into the core of that person and see a light shining. You will feel better every time you do it.

2. You go to the same church as a member of the school board who holds views that are diametrically opposed to yours. Your ego mind judges her and feels indignant. Every time you see her, you end up complaining to your husband later and building a case for how much she's hurting your community.

But when you tune into your higher mind and the light that you are, you relinquish judgment and adopt a neutral position about her, even though you still believe in your views. The next time you see her at church, you can say, "You know, we have some differences. But I respect you, and I'd like to understand your point of view better. Would you be willing to meet me for a cup of coffee?"

You have no idea how your life will be enriched by doing this. When your ego says, "What's the point? I've got laundry to do," remember that you are a representative of divine light.

Think of how valued the person will feel when you ask them. Think of how good the coffee will be. Think of the enlightening conversation you'll have. And maybe it'll lead to changes, common ground, a review of policies. Maybe it won't, but either way, you will expand the light in the world simply by listening.

The thing is, it's easy to judge from a distance, but not so much when you're face to face. So if you're assuming that someone is your enemy, do one thing: talk to him or her. The fastest way to make change in your world is to have a conversation.

3. You sit in the airport and people watch. Most of your internal commentary is something like: "Flip-flops? Really? It's winter. Didn't her parents teach her how to dress? Why are those parents letting their brats run around? I'd never do that with my kids."

When you do this, you judge yourself and heap that judgment onto others so your ego can make itself feel better. You're simply talking to yourself.

What does the light do instead? Strike up a conversation with the person next to you and see how quickly you can find a connection. Read something that makes you laugh. Watch the news on the airport TV and send love to everyone involved.

In other words, make better use of your time. Remember that the ego employs judgment as the justification and catalyst for everything we want to change, including violence, attack, shame, prejudice, and poverty. So if you find yourself fretting over the state of the world, take action by becoming aware of your own judgments. Then short-circuit them by asking for your fear-based thoughts to be healed and choosing the light that you are.

Here are a few things to remember about judgment:

- ❖ Self-love and judgment of others are mutually exclusive.

- ❖ If we judge, then our minds are in the lower world rather than higher ideals. We're focused on differences rather than oneness.

- ❖ Judgment reinforces a belief in separation and the Other.

- ❖ We are not equipped to judge anything. Our judgment of the homeless man on the corner makes him different from us, and we make assumptions based on his appearance. He may be our greatest teacher. When we judge, we miss the miracle.

❖ When we allow all things to be as they are, we allow a higher knowing to flow through us so we can see the gifts in every situation.

❖ The pain and fear and struggle and loneliness we feel in this life are there because we judge. Lay down judgment, and you can see peace instead.

❖ Judgment is the original fear, the cause of a belief in separation. It breaks people, things, and countries into separate pieces so we can say they're the "Other" and exclude them or feel superior. Those are all just attempts for our ego mind to feel better about itself.

❖ Judging what people wear or how they look is the same energy of separation that starts wars and creates riots. The more we focus on unity and peace in our own minds, the more we'll contribute to the larger world.

❖ You cannot judge others and feel good about yourself. Your ego may feel superior, but that's just temporary. The only way to practice Self-love and honor that in others is to know and remember the light that you are.

So what do you do when your ego *really* wants to judge? First, shift to your higher mind and the light within and say:

"I welcome our conversation."

"I see this as a way to move forward."

"I'll work with you to find common ground."

Then, if you need to, pour out your ego's anger in a letter you don't intend to send so you get it out of your system. This will allow you to speak from a more measured voice that people can respond to with kindness rather than fear.

Expect the best of others. I know it's entertaining to undermine and whine about a figure you love to hate. But it doesn't look good on the light of the world. Hold yourself to a higher standard—not because you're better than others, but because that's leadership, and because you're being true to who you are.

As you go through your day, see the light in people. See past their bodies. Say to yourself, "You are love and so am I."

As you do this, you'll find that you can lovingly detach. More about that in the next chapter.

six

Detach with Love

As you let go of judgment, you may feel like a burden's been lifted. But this is just the beginning.

By remembering the light that you are, you can free yourself of unhealthy entanglements—conscious and unconscious—that have been holding you back.

And as you do this for yourself, guess what? You do it for others, as well.

⌁

Picture this: You're sitting in your favorite chair at home. A piece of string connects you and the chair, symbolizing your attachment to it. After all, it belonged to your mom, and her mom, and her mom before that.

Other pieces of string attach you to your favorite coffee mug, your newest pair of shoes, and the high school yearbook boxed up in your attic. Now see a piece of string connecting you and your favorite person, plus the person you would *least* like to have lunch with.

Now there are strings connecting you with your favorite characters on TV, the websites you frequent most, and the go-to comfort foods in your refrigerator and kitchen cupboards.

Feeling a little tied up?

Just wait.

There are strings tying you to your favorite grocery store, all the apps you've downloaded, the newscasters you like most and least, and the public figures you love and love to hate.

Add a string for pets, loved ones, old friends, and the wedding photos on your dining room buffet.

And don't forget a string for every belief that makes you feel special, the restaurant you can't live without, and the song you listened to no less than a hundred times last month.

Tied down with all of these strings, getting up from your favorite heirloom chair and moving through your day is almost impossible—especially because you have hundreds if not thousands more strings tying you to everything, everyone, and every thought that you depend on for joy—and for blame.

It's important to point out that we aren't just talking preferences here. We're talking about the things, people, and belief systems that your ego believes are responsible for your happiness and unhappiness. For instance, the house that you're afraid to lose because it's part of your identity. The office you can't give up because it reflects your status. The friends you can't let go of because then you'd be alone on weekend nights. The unhappy marriage you stay in because you're afraid to find out who you are when you're on your own.

These are the attachments that complicate our lives and keep us stuck. They keep us all wound up, often in knots, as our ego tries to prove its value or find a safe harbor in life's storms. They are the sign of someone who has forgotten her own power and wholeness as the light of the world.

These special ego attachments single out another person or thing to make up for what you think is lacking in you. It's the *Jerry McGuire* "You complete me" scene come to life.

Here's how it works: I either project my guilt/shame/regret/anger/self-doubt onto you so I can feel better for a little while, or I set up expectations for your behavior. If you don't meet those expectations, my world falls apart, or I use you as an excuse to stay stuck. Some examples include:

- ❀ "My daughter flunked algebra. I'm so mortified."

- ❀ "The world is a mess, and it's all the Democrats'/Republicans' fault."

- ✿ "My husband forgot our anniversary. What will I do if he doesn't love me anymore?"

- ✿ "I'll never rest until my neighbor cleans up his yard."

- ✿ "I have to get that promotion at work or my family will think I'm a failure."

If you remember that you're the light of the world, does your happiness or Self-worth depend on the actions of others? No, because you *are* happiness. You *are* love. You *have* everything you need, and you *are* everything you need.

Think of it this way: A giraffe doesn't need a ladder, and a porcupine doesn't need a suit of armor. You come equipped with all the attributes and qualities you're looking for. And you'll find them inside you, not in other people's behaviors.

This doesn't mean that relationships aren't important. We're in these human bodies to be in relationship because that's how we extend love into the world. But when we interact with others through unhealthy attachments, we join our fear with their fear, holding them hostage for our happiness. When we interact from a place of Self-love, we join our light with their light, enjoying them as they are rather than how our egos want them to be.

So how do we detach without withdrawing from the world? Here are some essential things to remember first.

We get attached to people. When I was a little girl, I thought attaching was the smart thing to do. Attach to your toys and don't let anyone else play with them. Attach to friends and don't let anyone else in. Attach to your dog and keep her all to yourself. Growing attached in some ways is seen as healthy. We want to bond. We want to belong. We want to have something we can call our own.

Eventually, though, the ego's need to be loved supplants your belief in your Self, so you search for someone to care for you and make you feel good about yourself. Or your children grow up and start making decisions that could hurt them, so you step in and try to take control "for their own good." The world defines this as love, but it's actually motivated by fear.

You may be attached to a friendship that's not healthy, a family or cultural history that keeps you trapped in sorrow, a job that's stifling your creativity, and a paycheck that you think you can't live without, even though you head to work each morning with a feeling of dread in your stomach.

When these attachments eventually disappoint you, which they're bound to do, you're left scrambling for the next special relationships to prop you up and give your life meaning.

Until, that is, you remember to look inside at the light that you are. When you see that your needs have already been met—and always will be—by the unending supply of divine love, you can start to disentangle yourself from the web of needs your ego has said you can't live without.

We get attached to outcomes. Think about doctors and social workers. Every day they work with people who need healing, and every day they lose or gain more patients and clients. What would happen if they got attached to a specific outcome for everyone who came through their offices or clinics? They'd be crippled emotionally, buffeted around by the journeys and hurts and joys of others. To be effective, they have to find a balance between caring and detaching, knowing their patients and clients have their own journeys and lives to live. And most important, they know that outcomes are not always up to them.

Think of applying this approach to a family wedding, settling yor parents' estate, or sending your child off to college.

Your ego will try to control outcomes from its limited view of the situation. But the high Self trusts that the outcome will serve the highest good in the bigger picture.

When you detach with love . . .

- ❖ You don't hold anyone or anything responsible for your happiness.

- ❖ You spend less energy worrying about losing what you have and more time enjoying the people and blessings in your life.

- ❖ You trust Spirit to take care of things that you can't understand or fix.

- ❖ You don't hold onto grievances or keep reliving old stories.

- ❖ You don't take other people's decisions personally.

- ❖ You aren't buffeted around by other people's fears. You stand in your own light without worrying what other people think or mimicking the path that's right for them.

❖ You see the people in your life not according to their titles and relationship to you, but as the children of God and the light that they are. This erases expectations and unhealthy attachments because you respond to them with love, not the way a wife's love should look, or a mother's or a sister's. Those defined and limited forms of love are attached to the ego. This detached love flows from Source without definitions of what it should look like.

❖ You enroll in the "Bless and Release" program. Ask Spirit to enter in, bless someone or something in your life, then let go and know that you have spread your light.

How can you start detaching with love?

Place your entire future in the hands of God. At its core, this is the biggest lesson of detachment. Let go of thinking you have the answers. Surrender your ego's need to make decisions without the help of Spirit.

Why? So you can spend your life in the joy of the present moment instead of worrying about the future. In this place, we remember that we are one with God and our minds are healed.

Here's what I want you to do: Find a small box or bowl and set it in a special place in your home. Know that this container represents the hands of God.

Now cut up a sheet of paper into small pieces, about the size of a fortune from a fortune cookie. Set those small slips and a pen next to the container, and keep some of the slips with you wherever you go.

Each day as you find yourself thinking about the future—whether it's with excitement, anticipation, or worry—write down a couple of key words on one of the slips of paper. For instance, you might write down "Health insurance" or "Holiday gatherings" or "First day of work" or "Life as an empty nester." Just write enough to capture the essence of your thought about the future.

Now put the slips of paper into the container. Say to yourself, your guides and angels, and the Holy Spirit: "I place the future in the hands of God. I am worthy of all the blessings waiting for me."

Pay attention to any shifts you experience as you fill the container with everything you're entrusting to God. This is the true nature of detaching, freeing you to be the light that you are.

Follow this thought of loving detachment from the higher mind: "I trust that other people's soul growth is between them and God."

One of the ego's greatest tricks is to distract you from your own inner growth by pointing out what everyone else— including adult children, colleagues, best friends, and distant cousins—"should" be doing to live a more successful or happier life.

Your higher Self, on the other hand, recognizes that everyone has their own journey, which you may or may not understand. And, just like you, the people around you are in the more-than-capable hands of Spirit, who will support them in the way they need.

That's why your higher Self will always bring you very gently back to your own growth, focused on what's going on for you.

As you go through the day, repeat that thought to yourself—"I trust that other people's soul growth is between them and God"—especially if you feel your mind getting pulled into other people's drama. Bless those in your life, see the light in them, and ask for your own peace to be maintained so you can carry that peace with you wherever you go.

Practice what *A Course in Miracles* calls "true empathy." This is the ability to put your arm around the shoulders of people who are suffering but not get swept away by their pain. When you do this, you can affirm the light in them that they can't see for themselves.

Typically, we see empathy as walking in another person's shoes, which means identifying with her pain and struggle. This can often lead to commiserating with her about what a victim she is or what a lousy deal she got, amplifying the struggle.

But when you practice true empathy, you'll find yourself in situations where there's very little so say except "I believe in you. I know you can do this. I love you. How I can help?"

Listening to someone who is in a chronic spin cycle of fear isn't healthy for him or you. Retelling fear-based stories simply deepens a mental groove and blocks the light even more. So should you listen to someone's complaints or sorrows? Sure. There can be healing in the telling. But if you find the person stuck in her negative story, reminding her of the light within is the proper use of empathy.

You might say something like, "It sounds like things are really hard for you right now. But I know you'll find a way. There's no limit to the ways things can get better. You're more than these challenges."

When we can hold that space for others, we help them remember the light that they are and the strength they have within.

Know that detaching will feel uncomfortable at times. Your ego will chastise you and call you cold-hearted and unloving. It will want to rush in and rescue so it can feel better about itself. But that's putting the ego in place of trust and a greater power.

Should we help? Of course. But if you do it with the attachment of "I'm going to save the world," you'll get burned out, and you may interfere with a better, divinely guided solution. Similarly, if you try to force your beliefs on others—

such as pushing alternative health options on someone who believes in traditional medicine or vice versa—you may create more pain than comfort out of your need to be right. Help wherever you're called, but serve as the hands and feet of Spirit, not the ego.

Detach from things and from people when it's time to leave them behind, without holding on too long. You may have enjoyed second grade, but you don't stay there your whole life. You might have loved your red skinny jeans, but at some point you outgrew them. If we try to hold onto all the people and things in our lives because we think we'll hurt someone's feelings when we move on, we eventually are so dragged down by the energy that we can't move forward.

Detaching with love will help make sure you don't stay in relationships and jobs that no longer fit. I've manufactured all sorts of crazy reasons for moving on, as if the fact that "I don't want to be here anymore" or "I'm feeling stifled" or "You are not healthy for me" isn't enough. You don't need anyone's permission to know what's right for you. Be honest about what (or who) is dimming your light and what's making it shine brighter, then choose the path of Self-love.

"Practice 'true empathy'–
the ability to put your arm
around the shoulders of
people who are suffering
but not get swept away
by their pain. "

Detach from beliefs that no longer serve you. For instance, how often do we hear that acts of kindness are the exception rather than the rule? "People don't take care of each other anymore," the ego complains. "It's every man for himself."

Crises of all kinds bring out the best in people, but our egos overlook the fact that there are millions of people every day who are helping one another in quieter, less acclaimed ways than rescuing neighbors from flood or fire. You'll find evidence to support whatever you're looking for. By detaching from old beliefs, you can see the evidence of love.

Make a list of all the things and relationships you depend on for your sense of identity and happiness. Do they define you? No. If they went away, would you still be the light that you are? Yes. Even if you were stripped of everything in this physical world, you would still be the light.

Reach out and help someone without any expectations. Do it totally out of love, not out of trying to prove yourself by being the hero or attempting to fix his or her life.

Resist meddling in your own life. Instead of fixing or trying or controlling, sit still and see what Spirit can do.

Look at how many of your attachments are fueled by guilt. This requires an honest assessment, and you may be surprised at how much guilt you find because it can take so many different forms. For instance, you go to church because you'd feel guilty if you didn't. You volunteer in your child's homeroom because that's what you're "supposed" to do. You polish your heirloom silverware because your mom always did, even though you never use it and it just sits in a drawer.

As a wise friend said, guilt is an appropriate emotion if you've done something wrong. But most of the time, we feel guilty because we're not meeting others' expectations. In families, cultures, and religions, guilt goes a long way toward "keeping people in line." Ask yourself: "Where in my life am I letting guilt limit my light?"

What does detaching with love look like? Here are some examples.

1. You've had a prickly relationship with your mom for years because she's a chronic complainer. According to her, nothing in her life ever goes right. She gossips about people, complains about work, and even says negative things about your siblings behind their backs—which means she's saying negative things about you behind your back, too.

Your ego wants to tell her off and has a hard time being civil. Every conversation triggers memories of the past, and you end up fuming for hours after every phone call. You wonder, "Why me? Why did I get *her* for a mom when my friends have moms that they actually like?"

Now put on your detach-with-love glasses and look at the same situation through the eyes of Spirit. What does it look like from this perspective?

Your mom has been in the throes of fear for a long, long time. She's living out the ego beliefs of "I'm not lovable" and "The world is a scary place . . . You can't trust anybody."

Everything she says is a reflection of how she feels about herself and has nothing to do with you or anyone else. With love, you can detach from trying to fix her, rescue her, or buy into her pain.

You can also let go of any victim mentality and see that she has helped you become the person you are. You know that the best way to help is to send her love and healing via the

Holy Spirit, and to continue seeing the light in her, knowing she can't see it in herself.

If she needs you, you'll be there to help. But because of your own Self-love and respect, you don't need to engage in conversations that go nowhere, and you politely request a different kind of conversation with her. For instance, you might say, "Mom, I know things don't always go the way you'd like. But I'd really like to hear some of the positive things happening in your life." If she's not able to meet your request, you can decline the conversation, guilt free.

2. **Every time you read, hear, or watch the news, you feel overwhelmed and angry.** Another animal has become extinct, another teenager has committed suicide after being bullied online, another criminal has walked free because the Justice Department didn't do its job, or another terrorist attack has killed innocent civilians.

You can't see any way out of this mess, and you're sure the people in positions of power are just looking out for themselves. "Where are the leaders?" you wonder. "How is anything going to change?" You can feel your blood pressure rising and your

135

body tightening from stress. Then you remember Self-love and loving detachment, focusing on what's possible rather than what's not.

Can you save every animal and person on the planet? No, so you detach from that feeling of responsibility and helplessness and ask other questions instead. For instance, can you donate to a wildlife fund to support conservation efforts? Yes. Can you talk to the parents of your children's friends about monitoring bullying on their social media accounts? Yes. Can you write letters to your representatives about your views on legislation and international security? Yes.

You see that hopelessness is the ego's way of keeping us inert so we won't take positive steps. But when you detach from that fear and focus on what's possible instead, you take action— empowered, inspired, and guided by the light that you are.

3. Someone close to you is dying, and you need to let go. This may be one of the hardest applications of detachment, but it's also one of the most important. It means honoring their wishes, giving them permission to go so they can detach when they're ready, and accepting that we can't see the bigger picture.

A friend of mine knows two people with life-threatening diseases, and she talked with a healer about their prognoses. She learned that, for both her friends, the illnesses are serving an important soul purpose. For one, it's providing the exit from life she has wanted for quite some time. She's never felt valued in life, and in dying, the disease actually gives her a sense of control.

For the other friend, a slow-growing cancer in remission is a way of deepening his spiritual connection. It allows him to explore his spirituality in ways he couldn't do otherwise.

Both situations demonstrate that we make assumptions and assign meaning that may be far from the truth. And we assign labels of "good" or "bad" when we can't see the whole picture. When we lovingly detach, we allow soul growth to happen in its own way, serving the light rather than fear.

⁓

Remember: Detachment is not letting go of love. It is, in fact, acting from love that frees others rather than imprisoning them.

To detach with love, you'll be approaching situations in a way that may feel unfamiliar—with no past, no baggage, no judgment. With those barriers out of the way, you'll be free to see the deeper meaning and lessons within the situation. What gifts does the situation give you? How can you use it to grow?

When you clearly see the difference between the ego's vision and God's—and when you understand that you get to choose which set of eyes you're going to look through every day—you'll know that there's only one choice that makes sense.

No more need for struggle.

And with that, you'll be ready to rise above the battleground.

seven

Rise Above the Battleground

When you're no longer tethered by unhealthy attachments, you can rise above any situation, shine your light on it, and see it from a different perspective. This lifts you out of your frustrations and worries, which certainly makes life more peaceful. But it helps the world, too, because you're no longer contributing to the collective fear and chaos.

This is why we need to rise above the fear in our everyday lives, ask a higher power for help, surrender our attachment to being right, and, as much as the ego may protest, give up the fight.

———

A Course in Miracles describes the battleground of our lives as the drama, chaos, attack, and defense that take place in our minds and in our world every day. Imagine it as one enormous human chessboard that reflects what's going on in our thoughts, acted out in our homes, schools, and workplaces. It seems real, but it's simply a reflection of the skirmishes in our fear-based minds.

Everyone on that chessboard is trying to gain advantage over others, whether they want to take over a company or simply prove a point. The players are all trying to anticipate their opponents' next moves, their feelings, their moods, and when they might attack.

A person who grew up with an alcoholic parent knows how unpredictable the battleground can be. As a child, he may have learned to live under the radar so he wouldn't get caught in the crossfire.

A person who has worked for a tyrannical boss knows the intricacies of the battleground, too, where one minute she's the favorite and the next minute, she fears for her job.

But the battleground often is more subtle than this. It may be a marriage in which you don't feel appreciated, or a friendship based on a shared interest that falls apart when you realize you view the world in different ways.

In any case, the action on the human chessboard is an exhausting game, with your ego on high alert, scanning the constantly changing landscape and searching for clues. Are you safe? Who likes you? Who doesn't? Who can you please? Who will you disappoint?

Once your ego takes in all this data, it projects it back out. Your Aunt Sue has never liked your boyfriend, so you try to keep the two apart at family dinners. An old friend didn't send you a Christmas card this year, so you take her off your list for next year. Your state representative votes against a program you support, so you lambast him on social media. All of these actions create a closed-circuit loop of attack and defense that plays out over and over, seemingly with no escape.

But the battleground is not "out there." It's always in your own ego mind. Maybe Aunt Sue doesn't actually dislike your boyfriend, but you think she does because you're not so sure about him yourself. Maybe the friend didn't send you a card because she's decided to simplify her life, and it has nothing to do with her feelings for you. Maybe the representative had legitimate reasons for his vote, but your ego is invested in making him wrong.

In short, the world is not attacking you. You are attacking you.

And there is only one way out of it.

Let me say this again: There is only one way out. And that is to rise above and live from your higher mind.

When you do this, there's no longer a need for blame. No trying to figure out if there's something wrong with you

" The world is not

attacking you.

You

are attacking you."

or anyone else. No energy spent remembering past guilt or shame. You simply pause, remember the light that you are, and ask Spirit to lift you above the battleground, where the drama doesn't exist.

Let's look at four key elements of rising above the battleground.

It brings an end to the cycle of attack and defense. When you rise above the battleground, you remove yourself from the human chess game. You no longer feel like others are out to get you. And that means the government, education, your boss, your spouse, a friend doing something behind your back, an ex-spouse cheating on you. It removes the paranoia and replaces it with peace.

When you're on the battleground, you have a position to defend, and your "enemy" holds what seems to be an opposing position. This could be pro-gun versus anti-gun or pro-curfew versus anti-curfew. It could be defending the kind of pizza you want to order, which becomes a battle in your own mind—not over pepperoni versus sausage, but asking yourself why you always get what everyone else wants and why nobody cares what you want.

Your energies go into maintaining your position as a way of controlling the situation. But those attack thoughts teach you that you need to fear this cruel world—a belief that does more damage than we realize. Anything we use to "protect" ourselves—such as guns and war—actually weakens us. Why? Because light needs no protection. If we're bracing for a fight, then we're right back on the battleground, and we've forgotten what we are.

When you rise above the battleground, you can see the light in everyone, which allows you to love your "enemy." This is when truces are possible. When the fight ends.

To the ego, this is capitulation, to be avoided at all costs. Your ego mind will defend its place on the battleground out of pride, stubbornness, fear, and simply not knowing what else to do. But fortunately, when you rise above the battleground, you no longer focus on defending a position. You focus on the unifying power of love.

When you start to do this regularly, you develop a bigger vision. You stop being pulled into drama. You give up your place on the chessboard and lose interest in playing the game.

And when the ego puts its hands on its hips, stares you down, and says, "So what are you going to do now?" you can smile, go for a walk, and see how much better the world looks in the light.

Rising above the battleground allows you to give up the fight in your own mind. Your internal conflict may sound like: "How am I going to prove myself?" "What in the world did I do that for?" "Nobody really saw me when I was little, and I'm angry at myself for being invisible, even though I did it to stay safe."

So what's an example of giving up the mental fight?

Let's say you're struggling with an issue at work. You're trying to score points with your boss, but it seems like everything you do goes unnoticed. The fight is really not about your boss. It's about you feeling the need for outside affirmation to prove your worth.

You're engaged in a slugfest of your own making, even though the world around you supports it, and you're acting it out in the battleground known as "the office." Aren't we supposed to claw our way up the corporate ladder? Haven't we been taught that it's not an easy climb?

But the fight going on in your own mind is exhausting because no matter how many accolades you receive from your boss or coworkers, they'll never be enough. Even when it gets what it wants, the ego will fight on, finding another battleground, another clash.

In fact, in its paranoia of attack and defense, the ego is wary of love itself. That's why it looks on happiness, generosity, and caring with suspicion. "What's that person's angle?" it might say. "What's he trying to pull?"

This is when it's time to wave the white flag. Surrender is not a sign of weakness. It's a sign of strength because at this moment you stop trying to have all the answers and let yourself be guided instead.

And what happens then? You come home to your higher Self. You remember that you've been frantically trying to control circumstances around you, attempting to find your value through your ego, when it was never there to begin with.

You remember that the answers lie in what's right for *you*, and every time you trust what's for your highest good, it will be used for the highest good of all others as well.

You start being more honest. You use your energy to get your work done rather than trying to get attention. You're satisfied with your own efforts without needing the approval of others.

You lay down your sword. And as you do, you allow a higher power to direct your life. That's exactly when you probably *will* receive the notice your ego has been looking for because you'll no longer try so hard—an act of fear that kept what you wanted at bay.

The fight often happens when you're feeling crummy about yourself, because that's when the ego is determined to prove itself, or when it curls up in a fetal position and eats sour cream potato chips. That's not the kind of surrender we're talking about.

This kind of surrender acknowledges that you don't have all the answers—and don't need to. This immediately pulls you into the present moment because you're not looking to the past for explanations or to the future for outcomes.

Giving up the fight means laying down all need to be right, to prove yourself, to win, to be the victor, to be better than someone else. But it's not angry resignation that feels like "I'm not important, my feelings don't matter." Instead, it means living with trust. "I simply need to let my light shine and know it is enough."

Above the battleground, you let all things be as they are. When you rise above the battleground, you practice acceptance and patience, and you give people the time and space to do the right thing.

You let children grow up to be who they are by offering support and guidance, not rigidity. You listen to others as they have their say, knowing that being heard can lead to consensus. And you work with higher energies, following their guidance so you can experience the breakthroughs of fresh perspectives.

As you do this, you're saying to Spirit, "I don't have the answer to this, but I know you do. I put myself in your hands, and I will do my job, which is to receive your guidance and grace. I will speak with your voice, think with your mind, and see with your eyes."

When you rise above, you realize how much time you've spent worrying about nothing. Here's an example: A client of mine once read a news report about a couple nearing retirement. The couple had taken out student loans on behalf of their child, and they couldn't pay them back.

"I don't want that to happen to me," my client said.

The reality is that her children have graduated from college and, thanks to her wise financial planning, their educations are paid for. She and her husband have a nest egg, and they're still years away from retirement.

Their situation has nothing to do with the one in the report. It would be like saying, "I read a news article about a barracuda jumping into a boat in the Gulf of Mexico and eating the boat owner's Chihuahua. I don't what that to happen to me." The thing is, you don't own a boat, you never go fishing, and you don't have a Chihuahua. The likelihood of the first example happening is as remote as the second, yet the ego wants to worry about *something*. Otherwise, how will it prove its worth?

When you become aware of the many dramas you play out in the battleground of your own mind, you see how often you live in the future, polishing your suit of armor for conflicts that will never show up.

So let's talk about how you rise above the battleground. What's the practice?

Imagine that you're in the middle of a fight with your teenage daughter, and you ask Spirit to lift you out of the drama so you can see it differently. As you do, your inner vision changes, and you switch to your higher mind and spiritual eyes. This allows you to observe yourself and your daughter battling over her curfew and the fact that she's broken it again.

Instead of wearing a shield, feeling you have to stand your ground and make her behave, you can look at yourself and say, "Oh, look at that mom. She loves her daughter dearly and is so afraid for her daughter's safety. Plus, she's afraid she's messing up as a parent. She's afraid something will happen to her beloved girl and she'll never be able to live with herself because she'll believe that it's her fault, that she failed to keep her daughter safe.

"And look at that teenage girl. All hormones and independence and wanting to make her way in the world and prove she can be on her own. And inside she's just a scared little kid who really wants to be sheltered by her parents but feels like she doesn't deserve that level of love. And she can't forgive herself for messing up and being the 'bad seed' in the family, so she's going to keep acting out because she just can't let herself receive love. It's easier to say 'I hate you' than 'I love you' because she's not loving herself."

Imagine being able to not just see it all but *feel* it all. Both sides. The love and the fear. How both people are doing the best they can with those ego minds of theirs, even though they want to live from the mind of love.

And there you are, witnessing it all without judgment. No swords, no arrows. Just simple compassion.

Now imagine that you can speak from that compassion and big-picture vantage point

You might say, "We have a curfew because we love you and want you to be safe. I'll be honest and say that if anything happened to you, I would be devastated because I love you. And if I'm really honest, I know I couldn't live with the grief, and I couldn't live with blaming myself for letting something happen to you.

"So I'm enforcing this curfew for you—and for me, too. I know you want to be grown up and be the light that you are. Part of that is respecting the rules in this house and valuing yourself. Breaking a curfew makes it more likely that something could happen to you, and I don't want you in that position. And as much as your ego may love the drama, you don't want to be in that position either. This is not about whether I trust you or not. This is about all of us making smart decisions and respecting ourselves and each other."

That's a very different conversation than, "These are the rules, and you either abide by them or you're out."

Now, I'm not saying that rising above the battleground will always change things. But yes, it will.

You can do this same thing with any situation, any relationship. Rise above the battleground to see your ex-spouse through different eyes. Practice seeing from above the battleground at work. Watch the news and rise above it. Any time you feel yourself pulled into battle, take a breath and ask for Spirit to lift you up.

Remember: It's not your job to fix the world, just to bring your light to it. As my friend Dorothy used to say, "You can reach into hell to help someone, but don't ever go there yourself."

What does it look like to rise above the battleground? Here are some examples.

I. It's getting close to the holidays, and you can feel your internal stress starting to rise. You're going to be spending a long weekend with your family, and that means reliving a childhood filled with unhappy memories.

When you're on the battleground, you brace yourself for the attack. You put on emotional bubble wrap and hang out in the past, reliving difficult moments from a lifetime of contentious holidays. You start practicing comebacks so you'll be ready if you feel insulted or slighted. You're sorry that every year brings this same slow simmer of anger, but you don't know any other way to get through the holidays without bracing yourself for what's to come.

But when you rise above the battleground, you have a different perspective. You see everyone in the family as the light that they are. In fact, their roles as mother, father, and sibling fall away, and you see them simply as children of God, just like you.

You see that they've always been afraid and have worn their own battle garments, attacking and defending because they didn't know any better. But they're all tired of it, just like you. The only difference between you and your family is that you remember you're all the light, and they don't.

From your perspective above the battleground, you send love to each of them, asking for your light to bless theirs. You see that there's no separation between you, and that it's only the special attachments you formed that have kept you stuck in the dance of attack and defense all these years.

By detaching and seeing them from a different perspective, you free them to be who they are, knowing that the shame they directed at you was a reflection of their own fear. You free yourself to send them love. And while you're at it, you send love to the home where the holiday gathering will be so the energy and light will fill that space while you're all there.

2. Your husband has been diagnosed with cancer, and it feels like the rug has been ripped out from under you. From the minute you get the news, you're fully gripped by fear about his well-being, your financial future, grief at the prospect of losing your best friend, and how you'll raise your kids alone.

When you and your husband discuss treatment options with the doctor, you're on board to fight the cancer every step of the way, ready to attack it and defend your husband and family. You feel responsible for fixing it and making sure everyone is okay.

That means managing everyone's feelings, your husband's meds, and your own fears.

When you rise above the battleground, you have a very different perspective. Your grief and worry are mitigated by trust. You know that the cancer has a message for your husband—and for you as well. You find peace in pouring love onto the battleground for your husband, your children, and yourself. You even send love to the cancer and thank it for the gifts it's bringing, such as greater closeness in your family or the opportunity to talk about what matters most. You give up the fight—meaning the conflict in your own mind.

You and your husband talk about the cancer and what it can teach you. In one of those conversations, you learn that he has always worried about dying young and not walking your daughter down the aisle one day. Together, you ask for that fear to be fully healed, knowing this will support his body as well. The cancer is a sign of separation, so experiencing wholeness within himself is key for your husband, and for your entire family.

Instead of fighting the cancer, you love it as it is, and you feel the anxiety and stress settle down. Your husband follows the treatment plan, but now your focus is on love rather than attack. This creates an environment in which everyone—your kids included—can express their emotions and experience a shared peace. No more fight or flight. Simply light instead. Notice that the focus is not on the outcome in the future, but on the love right now.

3. You've spent the last six years helping to plant and maintain a community garden in your neighborhood. You and other volunteers have donated the produce to your local food bank and churches, and the space has become a safe place for neighbors to gather.

Now the city wants to turn the land into commercial property and open it up to development. You and the other volunteers know this will severely impact people who rely on the garden for fresh food, and it could destroy the neighborhood's sense of community.

Your ego is ready for battle and immediately blames the "money-grubbers who don't care about regular people." In doing so, you put yourself in a position of defense and attack and make yourself feel powerless. How could you possibly win a battle against the city?

So you rise above the battleground. You ask Spirit to give you a different perspective. You imagine yourself looking down on the garden and the people involved from a different vantage point so you can see the situation as an opportunity rather than a fight with a victor and loser. You trust that, with the support of Spirit, possible outcomes are limitless.

From this more neutral place, you can talk with the other volunteers and city leaders from a position of common ground. This doesn't lessen your passion, but now your sense of purpose is fueled by light instead of fear. It allows you to ask questions like:

- ❀ "What does the garden bring to the neighborhood?"

- ❀ "What would commercial development bring to the neighborhood?"

- ❀ "What do we value?"

- ❀ "What can we all agree on?"

- ❀ "Is the solution all or nothing? Could the commercial development include a garden space? Could the garden space include room for business?"

- ❀ "What's the best way for this decision to be made?"

- ❀ "How can neighbors have a voice?"

From above the battleground, the outcome is likely to be more conciliatory and inclusive. Most of all, it changes what's inside you from "I'm never going to win. The world is against me" to "I show up in my life as the light that I am." And that's a win-win for everybody.

Here are a few other things to know about rising above the battleground.

- ❀ The fear-based thoughts that create the human chess game are the same whether the chessboard is your household or global politics. Rising above the battleground works in every situation, "small" or "large," because it always starts in your mind.

❖ When we're on the battleground, solutions can seem limited. For instance, if you're trying to find a job in a tight market, you might feel discouraged even before you start, thinking the odds are against you. But when you rise above the battleground, you remember that your resume and networking skills aren't the only things working on your behalf. Spirit is the true source of what you want, and it has already lined up the perfect job for you, even though you can't see it yet. Best of all, because your fears aren't standing in the way, a higher power can lead you to that perfect position—or deliver it to you when you least expect it.

❖ The consequences of rising above the battleground include having more patience, more understanding, and gently helping other people see what you see— not one right answer, but the light that they are.

❖ When you rise above the battleground, you see your purpose differently. The goal is not to win, but to grow together with others, creating more unity in the world. Instead of feeling like you don't belong, you realize you fit in everywhere because you no longer have to do or say the right thing to preserve your place on the chessboard. Instead of worrying whether you'll understand people in another country or another neighborhood or of another color, you rise above the battleground and see that love is a universal language.

❀ Rising above is not done out of moral superiority. It's not a contest to determine who is the bigger person or who takes the higher road. Instead, this rising above disengages you from battle and offers you a different and more expansive view.

❀ By making an assessment of your life, you can identify the different chessboards your ego has set up on your behalf. To find them, ask yourself, "In what part of my life do I feel like I'm always fighting for or against something? When do I feel defensive? When do I want to lash out? What games am I playing with myself and others that feel old and worn out?" Once you've spotted the battlegrounds, ask for your fear-based thoughts to be healed so you can withdraw your troops and experience the freedom that peace provides.

These thoughts and words will lift you above the battleground.

* To Spirit: "I don't know how to handle this, but I know you do, so I'm handing it over to you and trust that you'll resolve it for the highest good."

* To a person who is mired in fear: "I know you've been struggling with this for quite a while. How about if we look at it a different way?"

* To a person who approaches life differently than you do: "I appreciate your point of view. Thank you for helping me expand my thinking and consider a different perspective."

* To yourself and Spirit, when you're experiencing self-doubt: "I know there's a better way. Please help me see this through the eyes of love."

* To a person who is attacking you: "I'm sorry you're having a rough time. Let me know if I can help."

❀ To yourself when you're tired, and you feel yourself drawn back to the battleground: "I'm going to go for a walk/take a nap/go get some coffee/read for a while so I can remember the light that I am."

From above the battleground, you see unity rather than separation. You see light rather than darkness. You see everyone free of their roles, their arrows, and their shields.

You see the gossiping coworker as a young woman who is afraid of her own power. You see your passive-aggressive friend as a child who always felt invisible. You see your hapless son trying to meet other people's expectations rather than listening to his higher Self.

This doesn't mean you give up on people. To the contrary, it means that you see the light in them with true empathy and hold that space for them when they can't see it for themselves.

With this bird's-eye view—and an intention to bring more peace to your world—you're ready to solve life's problems in a whole new way.

eight

Redefine the
Problem

Does it ever seem like the problems in the world are going to swallow us up? There are so many of them—financial, environmental, relationships, and health issues. They seem too numerous to count.

So what if we've just been programmed to see many problems and to feel overwhelmed by them, but we can change that conditioning from our perspective above the battleground?

What if I told you that, according to *A Course in Miracles*, there's only *one* problem and *one* solution?

And what if I said that, whether you want to legislate social change or simply get your kids to hang up their clothes, this principle works?

Don't believe me? Let's take a look.

⟶

Here's the *Course*'s take on it: Everything that we see as a problem in our lives comes from the same root fear: a belief that we're separate from God. The one solution to that problem is to remember we can never *be* separate from God. Nor can we be separate from ourselves or one another.

How does this relate to solving a problem? Here's an example.

Let's say your grown daughter expects you to take care of her son on a moment's notice. As much as you love your daughter and your grandson, you have other activities on your schedule. But you've said yes enough times that now your daughter assumes you'll always help her out.

It seems like the problem is your daughter and her expectations, but it's actually you. You've acted from the fear of disappointing her, of not being a "good" grandma, of creating conflict. This is a belief in separation because it comes from ego fear—the part of your mind that thinks it's separate from God and doesn't matter. But to disguise this belief as love, you set up those expectations, wrapped them in a bow, handed them to her, and said, "Here you go."

As soon as you remember that you're one with God, deserve Self-love, don't have to "earn" love from anyone, and gain a different perspective from your vantage point above the battleground, you'll respect the light that you are and set reasonable boundaries with your daughter.

"I'm happy to help when I can," you might say, "but there are times when I'll need to say no. Thank you for understanding." She might *not* understand—at least not right away. But when she realizes you're standing by your decision, she'll make other arrangements. "Problem" solved.

Here are three important things to know about the reality of one problem/one solution.

The source is the same. As we've gone through this book, some of the examples or scenarios may have seemed little, while others seemed big.

But here's what we need to remember: Anything that comes from fear is coming from the same fear, whether it's an offhand comment or an assassination.

This is important because until we really get this, our egos will continue to excuse some acts or words of fear because they "weren't that bad" and "we've got much bigger problems in the world." It seems that way because our egos are busy naming and cataloguing a whole host of problems.

For instance, facing a deadline at work seems different than a hurtful comment from a friend, which seems different than identify theft, which seems different than political parties withdrawing funding from a public program that feeds you. But they're all the same thing.

This is a big concept to get your head around, but it's essential to stop seeing other people as the root of our problems and recognize the true source. We have to know that the only "enemy" is the belief we all carry that we're not enough. And from that spring countless forms of shame, blame, anger, anxiety, judgment, and other forms of fear. A whole litany of "problems," all growing from the same roots, all of which can be solved by remembering the light.

"Well, that's different" doesn't exist. Think of how many times you've had conversations in which you or someone else has said, "Well, that's different." For instance, a minimum wage worker at a restaurant takes home a package of meat that was going to be thrown out, and he's fired for stealing. The CEO of the same company uses corporate money to buy a boat, and it's seen as a business expense. "Well, that's different."

A politician you support lies about campaign contributions and you make exceptions, saying that's just part of the job. A politician from the other party lies about the same thing. "Well, that's different."

" It's essential to stop seeing other people as the root of our problems and recognize the true source . . ."

Any time you hear yourself saying or thinking, "Well, that's different," stop yourself. You're making up reasons to expect more of one person and less of another. To let one person off the hook and hold a grudge against another. To say one person can do no wrong and another can do no right.

Those responses all come from your ego mind, which actively categorizes people as friend or foe, creating instant and lasting separation. The thing is, we base those labels on people's preferences and fears, not on who and what they really are. So whether you're taunting kids on the playground when you're in third grade or demonizing an entire political party as an adult, your ego is aligning itself with one group so it can actively judge and exclude another. The separation seems real. And "problems" arise.

For instance, I tend to vote a liberal ticket, and my husband votes a conservative one. We could define this as a problem in all sorts of ways. His views are wrong, or mine are. The two-party system is a train wreck. The other party has lost touch. But the real problem isn't who's right and who's wrong. It's that we believe our views can be separate, that we're separate, that we can work against each other.

What's the solution? To remember we can never be separate from ourselves, one another, or a higher Source. We can never be separate from love. Light cannot oppose light.

So what happens if one or both of us rise above the battleground and we approach the problem with the idea that we're on the same team even though we have different views? This is very different than the ego's win-lose mentality. Whenever we identify with Team Humanity rather than a territorial fragment of it, we quickly arrive at the common ground and bipartisanship where peace can be found.

There is no separation between you and your Self, other people, and God. Maybe you feel separate from a natural flow of abundance. You feel separate from your own desires. You feel separate from the potential clients you can help. And you feel separate from any sources of support, either human or spiritual.

The real problem is the belief that you could be separate from yourself, others, or a higher Source. The truth is, you can't be separate from any of those, so the solution, instead of looking in the physical world, is to look at what's true and lasting.

What's true and lasting is love, trust, spiritual support, and connection. So draw on those. Spend time each day reconnecting to your Self, Spirit, and others. Reach out to people who can support you and give you ideas. Spend time each day in meditation or reflection, working with your personal guidance system and trusting it's working on your behalf.

In other words, when problems come along, we tend to isolate and hide because we're afraid of being seen as a failure, and because our ego mind doesn't really want to succeed anyway. Yet that's exactly when we need to become clear about what we want, reach out, establish connections, and remember that we are the light—and so is everyone else.

How do you build the practice of seeing one problem and one solution?

❋ Whenever you have a problem, do whatever will bring more wholeness to it. First, remember that you're not separate from God, and ask for spiritual help. Ask what you need right now and listen for the answer. Ask for support and new perspectives. Remember you're not separate from your Self, so go within and ask what would be the highest expression of your love and light in this situation. No matter the answers you receive, taking the steps to feel your connection to Spirit, others, and your Self will bring you into alignment with love and make the solution easier to manifest.

❀ Know that fear divides, and love multiplies. If you feel you have a shortage of money, health, relationships, or success—whatever it might be—focus on the love within you and Source energy to multiply it. Ask for your fear-based thoughts about it to be healed, then focus on extending love.

For instance, if you think there's only one way for money to show up in your life, you're living according to ego programming rather than love. Maybe your ego says, "I can only make money through my job" or "The kind of money I want could only come to me if I won the lottery or someone died." Your high Self, on the other hand, remembers that divine love is your source, and divine love is unlimited. Focus on multiplying the loving energy of money and let God present it to you in a myriad of ways.

❖ Make a list of five "problems" in your life, then trace them back to the root fear. How are they all related to a belief in separation? How can remembering that you're one with God help you deal with the problem differently?

❖ Make a list of what you want and what you don't want in any situation. For example, at home, maybe you want some quiet time, everyone to pick up after themselves, and to sit down as a family for dinner at least once a week. Maybe you don't want bickering, feeling like you have to do laundry every day and take out the trash. Take a look at your lists from the standpoint of one problem/one solution. How is unity the answer to all your "problems," and how can you build it in your family?

❖ Ask the questions, "What's the kindest thing I could do for someone? What's the kindest thing I could do for myself?" These questions will heal the belief in separation, restore your memory of the light in you and others, and take the focus off the form of the problem and redirect it toward the solution. Those questions work in every situation, with every problem.

They work even for problems over which you think you have no control. For instance, nuclear arms. What's the kindest thing you can do right now for yourself around that problem? Ask for your fears about global destruction to be healed, knowing they are no more or less important than your fears about your children's grades or your elderly mother's dementia. What's the kindest thing you can do for another? Ask for love to pour into every country with nuclear arms, along with the heart of its leaders. Your ego will say this is not enough. But what could be more powerful and effective than summoning the unlimited help of Spirit to unify instead of divide?

❀ Ask yourself if anything in your life feels out of balance or is not a fair exchange.

For instance, if you feel like you're not being paid properly for your services, you need to bump up your rates, ask for a raise, or negotiate a different agreement. Otherwise, you're not practicing Self-love, and you're allowing your life to be out of balance because you believe you're not worthy.

If you're taking care of everyone else's issues and not tending to your own, you're not making an even exchange. If you're staying late at work to finish a project and someone else is taking credit for it, it's not an even exchange. The imbalance will affect other areas of your life, too.

Look at your life impartially. Maybe there's too much work and not enough leisure. Too much time with others and not enough alone time to recharge your batteries. Too much spending and not enough income.

Recognize that the problem is always the same: a belief that you're separate from your Self, God, and others. When you remember you're all part of the same indivisible light, you'll realize that being fair to your Self is the same as being fair to others. The balance in your life will be a symbol of unity, not separation.

❖ Ask for what you want and need, and trust that you'll be supported. For instance, maybe you want to reschedule an appointment so you have time to finish a project without stress. Your ego immediately jumps to separation. "What will he think of me if I cancel?" The real question is, "What will I think of myself if I don't ask for what I need? What will I teach myself about my own value?" When you ask for what you need, you claim your own value. And when you claim it for your Self, you affirm it for all others.

What does it look like in real life to understand that there's one problem and one solution? The following illustrations show how you can apply this principle to everyday life situations.

1. You've gained weight since you had your kids, and it's not coming off. When you look in your closet, you get angry, depressed, and ashamed. "Nothing fits," you say to yourself. Your inner dialogue spirals down from there. "I'm ugly. Look at those rolls of fat. How did I let this happen? I'm not who I used to be anymore. I don't want anyone to see me."

It's clear that you feel separate from yourself. You see a different body than you used to, so it seems like you're a different person. Plus, you blame yourself, feeling guilty and ashamed.

How do you believe you're separate from others? You don't meet the expectations of how the world says you should look. You don't want others to see you. You think you can hide and that you don't deserve to be seen.

And how do you believe you're separate from a higher Source? You believe you deserve to be punished. You think you are your body. You forget that this is not who you are. You forget that you are the light.

How does remembering that's there's only one solution—that we're all one and you are the light—solve the "problem"?

It solves the problem of separation from yourself because you can look at your body and feel love and compassion for it. Your body does not define you. It's simply a vessel that you're using while you're here. When you know that your identity and Self-worth don't depend on what your body looks like, you can detach and take care of it without the emotional fears. You believe you're deserving of love, so your body is free to come into balance at a weight that's healthy for you.

It solves the problem of a belief in separation from others. Because you're no longer judging yourself, you don't feel judged by the world. You can be comfortable in your own skin because you have gifts to share, not because of a number on a scale.

And it solves the problem of a belief in separation from a higher Source. You remember that you are the light of the world, not your body. There is nothing to be ashamed of, because there's no shame in divine love. As the light, you deserve health, well-being, and happiness. And those are not dependent on how much you weigh.

2. You're asked to join a community group, but the first meeting makes you squirm. You believe in the cause, but you aren't comfortable with the tone of blame and anger in the conversation. You say nothing because these are people you admire, you're new, and you don't want to rock the boat.

You feel separate from yourself through thoughts like, "I'm not enough. I don't have a right to speak up. And maybe they're right and I'm wrong."

You believe you're separate from others because you fear they may judge you. "I want to belong to this group, and they may kick me out if I disagree."

You believe you're separate from a higher Source when you think, "I'm not important enough for my opinions to matter."

When you remember there is no separation, you rise to your higher mind. You draw on the most important relationship you have: The one with your Self and a higher power. You ask your inner guidance for healing energy to flow through you and into the room. And you ask for your fear-based thoughts to be healed.

This gives you confidence to speak up with clarity and say, "I'd like to respectfully offer a different point of view." You do this without attachment to the outcome, asking for your words to be used for the highest good. Your focus is no longer on being ostracized by others, but on remembering the most important thing of all: to be true to your Self. When you do this, you make a stand for unity simply by being who you are.

3. Your next-door neighbors are building a shed that changes your view of the green space behind your house. You're sure they never gave a thought about how this would affect others, and you wonder if your property value will suffer. Every time you look at it, you feel your blood pressure going up.

How do you feel separated from yourself? Your ego feels like it has no control, and the shed seems like a personal attack. You feel separated from your neighbors because they're now the enemy. And you're forgetting your oneness with a higher power by thinking that your house, your neighborhood, and your property value dictate who you are and your happiness.

So how do you find a solution? Honor your Self by laying down your sword, rising above the battleground, and speaking with your neighbors as though you're on the same team. Don't simply try to pretend that the shed is okay with you, because your ego will continue to feel resentful. Instead, find out what the shed means to your neighbors and how they're going to use it. Look for a way to make it a win-win. Maybe if you help them paint it, they'll let you store your lawnmower in it over the winter. Maybe you could find as much beauty in the relationship as you do in the view.

It's hard to be angry over something you've invested yourself in, just as it's hard to bomb countries where your relatives live. So probe to find some common ground, then ask Spirit to use your conversation—and the shed itself—for the highest good of all.

Knowing that unity is always the solution allows you to address problems with a quiet but clear voice of conviction. Think of the Freedom Riders, who protested without violence. Before boarding buses and being delivered to the deep South, they prepared themselves to respond with peace, knowing they might be beaten and jailed.

Think of Rosa Parks, who simply refused to give up her seat on a bus. Think of Gandhi, who stood up to the British empire. Civil unrest does not demand throwing bricks through windows or upsetting cars and lighting them on fire. The voice of fear is loud and insistent, but it's the quiet, small voice—speaking from unity rather than separation—that penetrates the chaos and makes us pay attention.

Because everything is connected, solutions may appear where you least expect them, and divine forces will bring life into balance. For instance, if someone owes you money, doesn't pay, and disappears, talk to Spirit about it. Send love to the person who "cheated" you, then look for abundance to present itself in other surprising ways. When you remove the barriers of anger and blame, abundance is free to flow through you because of the light that you are.

In fact, every problem can be addressed on the level of spirituality, Source, light, and the higher mind rather than the ego trying to fix or control it in the world of form. Start with love first and use that to direct the solution with unity.

Then, when you know there's only one problem and one solution, you're ready to move on to forgiveness.

But, wait, because this is a different kind of forgiveness than you've ever seen before.

nine

Practice True Forgiveness

As you read in the last chapter, it appears that there's no end to the different shapes and sizes of problems. The same could be said for endless forms of hurt, attack, and betrayal—the stuff that can cause us to hold a grievance and a grudge and get in the way of forgiveness.

But when you understand that there's only one problem—a belief that we're separate from ourselves, one another, and Spirit—it means that there's only one thing we ever need to forgive: a belief that we're separate from ourselves, one another, and Spirit.

This one act of forgiveness changes *everything*.

So what if I told you we've been thinking about forgiveness and defining it all wrong? What if I told you that forgiveness has nothing to do with the person who hurt or betrayed you, and everything to do with you loving yourself?

What if I said that, more than anything else you can do to be the light that you are, this new definition of forgiveness will deliver you there at warp speed?

Hopefully this would help you take a second look at forgiveness. Because typically when we say the word *forgiveness*, it touches the deepest part of the ego, whose first response is either a sullen or belligerent, "No way. Not doing that." That's because we see forgiveness as letting someone else off the hook, which is the last thing the ego wants to do. The ego is all about making ourselves and others pay for our actions. That's how it keeps us believing we're separate, judging each other, attacking and defending, and forgetting the light that we are.

So let's look at forgiveness through this example, which is another reminder of why knowing you're the light and practicing Self-love are the bedrock of these ten principles and a peaceful life.

Lori has a three-year-old daughter, and she's insecure about her parenting habits. As a first-time mom, she always second-guesses her decisions and wonders if she's forever scarring her child with bad parenting. Her husband, Ryan, tries to reassure her, telling her she's doing a good job, but Lori's insecurity persists.

When Lori receives a job offer, she takes the position, knowing the extra money will help build a college savings fund. But she feels guilty about leaving her child.

Her mother says to her, "What are you thinking? You've got a daughter to take care of at home. How can you possibly be a good mom and hold down a job, too?"

Lori, who is already feeling insecure, now feels betrayed and attacked in a new way.

From this position on the battleground, she might launch her own attack. She might take out her guilt on Ryan. Or she might not say anything and let the hurt eat her up over time.

At some point she'll either decide to forgive her mom or she won't. And if she does, it'll probably be from the place of, "I don't think she really meant to hurt me, so I'll forgive her, even though it still hurts." The point is that Lori perceived her mom's comments as an attack because an arrow hit Lori right in the ego and lodged itself there.

Now let's imagine it a different way.

Lori is a first-time mom, and because she remembers the light that she is, she trusts her Self, Spirit, and her husband to do the right thing for their child and their finances. Lori isn't always 100 percent sure of her decisions, but she loves her Self enough to know that she's doing her best, and she can trust that she and Ryan know how they want to raise their child. They're not always perfect, but they have loving intentions, and Lori is secure about that.

When Lori decides to take a job, she harbors no guilt about it. She's clear about why it's the right decision for her and her family. Then one day her mom calls and says exactly the same thing as the previous example: "What are you thinking? You've got a daughter to take care of at home. How can you possibly be a good mom and hold down a job, too?"

This time, Lori's reaction is quite different. Even though her mom launched the same arrow, there was no target to hit. Her mom's comments went nowhere. Lori, feeling confident and at peace about her situation, could see that the comments had nothing to do with her and everything to do with her mom's own insecurities and guilt over the way she parented *her* children.

Because Lori had done the work of Self-love and loving detachment, there was nothing to forgive, because nothing really happened. Her mom simply made comments that had no power at all.

What's the core difference between the two examples? Not the external circumstances or situation. Those were the same in both examples. The difference was Lori's Self-love, which made her invulnerable to attack.

So here's the clincher:

Forgiveness is not about forgiving what happened; it's about forgiving a lack of love in ourselves.

In fact, any time we're hurt or feel betrayed, we're being given an opportunity to see where and how we can love ourselves more.

Okay. Take a breath. This is a profound reversal of thinking. So if your ego is jumping up and down and waving its arms right now, ask to be lifted above the battleground, where you can feel the love.

Here are some essential elements of this true forgiveness.

Forgiveness is the engine that keeps everything else on track. When our egos cling to old wounds, we can't see that the only thing holding us down is our own mindset. If you've ever felt persecuted, abused, or betrayed, you know how out-of-control your ego can be. One minute it may fume or rage over the way you were treated or what was stolen from you. The next minute it can fall into despair, wondering if you'll ever be happy again or how you can exist in such a hurtful world.

This is why true forgiveness is the most potent act of love. It wipes the slate clean. It doesn't just restore what you lost. It reminds you that who and what you are could never be lost in the first place.

This understanding is the ultimate threat to the ego, so it makes sense that whenever you think of forgiveness—even though it has the greatest potential to bring you peace—your ego will vehemently argue against it. For instance, it might say . . .

❧ *What do you mean you're going to forgive? After what that monster did to you?*

❧ *Don't let them off the hook. You deserve to be angry.*

❧ *Let him have it. It's the only way he'll learn.*

❧ *You'll never be able to live with yourself if you forgive her.*

❧ *This has been going on for generations. No way am I going to let it go.*

These messages are like heroin to the ego, which desperately wants to hold a grudge and keeps seeking opportunities to get a fix. Not surprisingly, this addiction to blame takes a toll on you long term. It keeps you stuck, holding onto negative and fear-based inner dialogues and relationships that diminish you and turn peace into an impossible dream.

True forgiveness is never about the other person. It's about our own Self-love and the meaning we give to an event. Here's an example:

My first marriage ended when my husband became involved in another relationship. Easy to blame my husband, right? But when I was honest with myself, the real hurt was that I didn't value myself enough to marry someone who had a higher regard for me. I needed to forgive myself for not valuing myself from the beginning.

And when I could see that I learned some valuable lessons from the experience, and that our divorce launched me into a period of massive Self-growth, the meaning I gave to it changed. Did I need to forgive my ex-husband . . . or thank him?

So here are two bedrock things to know about forgiveness:

I. The experience of "attack" and your response to it
    will change depending on how you feel about yourself.

2. The decision to hold a grudge or forgive is not about the external event. It's about your interpretation of the external event.

This doesn't mean that if you love your Self, nothing "bad" will ever happen. Or that, if you don't love your Self, it's your fault if you get hurt. These principles must never be used to blame yourself or anyone else. If they are, you're back on the same old battleground.

The truth is, the more we love ourselves and operate as the light in this world, the less likely we are to engage in attack and defense. And if you're not magnetizing that energy, your external circumstances are likely to calm down. It's like Prozac for the soul.

The more we live from our own light and the less we prescribe what other people's words and actions "should" look like to make us happy, the less need we'll have for forgiveness, and the easier it will be to forgive when a situation does come up.

You can forgive *and* set boundaries at the same time. You can forgive someone who hurt you *and* choose not to have them in your life. You can forgive *and* make it clear that there are consequences for unacceptable behavior.

Forgiveness is not:

- ❧ Letting yourself be walked on or taken advantage of.

- ❧ Accepting anger or abuse of any kind.

- ❧ Staying in a situation that's unhealthy emotionally, physically, or spiritually.

For instance, if someone accosts you physically or verbally, you can call the police *and* forgive him. If your mom is tearing you down, you can refuse to listen to her negativity *and* forgive her. If a coworker is uncooperative, you can talk to your boss about correcting the situation *and* forgive the coworker.

Remember: This boundary-setting works with Self-forgiveness, too. For instance, if you're working on losing weight and your ego keeps sabotaging you, it's absolutely okay to speak to your ego directly: "I forgive you, but you're not in charge. From now on, you don't get to choose what I put in my body. I will ask my higher Self and the Holy Spirit to make those decisions so I can choose foods that are for my highest good."

The interesting thing is that, once you forgive, the situation will likely improve because you've changed the dynamics. But if it doesn't, remember that Self-love is at the core of your inner peace. Forgive *and* take the action you need to create peace in your corner of the world.

Forgiveness wipes the lantern clean. Think about what happens when you feel slighted or hurt. The first thing your ego wants is to cut ties with that person.

Sour grapes, right? And what happens? You end up suppressing your light rather than beaming it out to the world.

For example, a family member snubs you at a holiday party, and you hold a grudge, saying, "Fine. If she's going to be that way, I just won't speak to her anymore." The result? You shut down part of yourself.

Or your business partner vetoes one of your suggestions. "Fine," your ego says. "If that's how it's going to be, then I won't get so excited about building this business anymore. If she doesn't appreciate me, maybe I won't offer any new ideas at all."

These situations seem petty, but they're very real. We all like to think we're more grown up than this, but egos are not known for their maturity. Forgiveness, on the other hand, gives you wisdom beyond your years.

Forgiveness is the revolution we need. If you asked a random sampling of citizens how a school shooter should be punished, a good share of them likely would say, "I hope he rots in hell. Execution would be too good for him."

An eye for an eye. It's seen as a reasonable response to a heinous crime.

But as we see more people speaking out about crimes like school shootings, we're witnessing a revolution toward legislation and school safety.

Just think how complete that revolution would be if compassion for the shooter were part of it. Think of how rooted in the light that would be.

Stopping short of forgiveness is like driving all the way across the country to get to the Grand Canyon, but then pulling off the road twenty miles before you reach your destination and visiting a museum about the Grand Canyon instead. It's a poor substitute for the real thing.

So if we want real change, then let's make real change.

Think about it this way: When the Holy Spirit looks at a school shooter, He sees light covered up under a blanket of darkness. He doesn't see evil or brokenness. He sees amnesia about the truth, caused by deep loneliness and pain.

There are all sorts of outcomes from trying to block out the light, and school shootings is one of them. But the act that needs forgiveness isn't the shooting, it's the fact that we forget what we are and act from fear rather than love.

We all do it. We all contribute to it. If we're on the battleground in our own minds, if we're berating ourselves or others in our minds, if we're insisting that our way is the right way and everyone else better get on board, we're contributing to a more chaotic world. And violence will be a part of that, no matter how much gun legislation we have.

We need to ask ourselves: "How could we have built a world in which a young person feels so desperate and angry that he would take violent action toward others? What's going on in our collective minds to make this possible? How can we bring wholeness to the situation rather than erecting more walls?"

Our ego minds are afraid—not of violence, but that we're not enough. And as long as we keep acting and thinking and living from fear, we'll have more anger and desperation.

So forgive whatever your fear-based mind is holding onto. Forgive yourself for forgetting what you are and the light that is in everyone else, too.

If you want to start a revolution, find someone to forgive.

Forgiveness is the one path to peace. To operate for the highest good as the light of the world, you want and need to be at peace. Holding onto any grievances or grudges throws dirt on your light and seems to dim it. Plus, it's a distraction for you because your ego keeps using up valuable energy by reliving the hurt.

Just think how often you replay a betrayal in your mind, and how often you replay a joyful moment or compliment. Chances are that the hurt is on continuous play, while the compliment or happiness is a one-time memory.

But when you forgive, you shift that balance. You're no longer on the battleground, and you see the truth of the slings and arrows: They have no real power to hurt you.

"Forgiveness

is the one path

to peace."

Imagine a target with a dozen poison arrows pointed at it. If you take the target away, they fly aimlessly and land on the ground, impotent. The takeaway is not, "Don't be a target" or "Don't make yourself a target." Instead, it is, "Love your Self enough to know there is no target."

Forgiveness frees us from the past. We've all heard the saying that we remember history so we won't repeat it. But is that true? Or are we keeping it present and unforgiven by remembering it and revisiting it over and over?

So far, remembering the Holocaust hasn't stopped genocide. Remembering World War I didn't prevent World War II. Remembering slavery hasn't kept society from suppressing people's rights or treating them as though they're indentured.

I'm not suggesting that we forget history, but that we forgive it so we truly can move on. Only then will we be less likely to recreate the same fears that have kept us stuck in those patterns of attack and oppression for so long.

How do we do this? We could start here: "For generations, we've all lived from our fears, hurting others as well as ourselves. Some of those hurts have seemed beyond forgiveness because they caused such deep pain for so many people—pain that has been carried on year after year. I don't want to suffer that pain anymore, and I don't want anyone else to, either. I know that building our world on anger and blame simply brings us more anger and blame, but when we forgive, a new world is possible. My desire for that peaceful new world—starting in my own heart—is greater than my desire to relive old wounds. And so I'm willing to forgive, and to be forgiven, asking that my light be used for the highest good. Please heal any fear-based thoughts that would keep me stuck in the past so that I can forgive completely, wiping the slate clean. Amen."

How do you build the practice of this new form of forgiveness?

* **Spend at least five minutes a day in conversation with Spirit.** Express your desire for peace, as a friend of mine says, in *your* little corner of the world, and then ask for any fear-based thoughts about forgiveness to be healed. This will help prepare your inner landscape for the peace you most desire.

- **Use the following mantra daily.** "I forgive myself and everyone on the planet in this moment—all moments in the past and in the future—for everything we have or have not done, said, felt, or believed. I recognize that everything is love or a call for love, and I forgive everyone, including myself, for any thoughts, words, or actions that have come from fear. I affirm the light in myself and all others."

- **Look for stories of forgiveness every day.** Is there someone you admire because of his or her ability to forgive? What words would you use to describe that person? How do you feel when you're around him or her? Can you think of a time when you truly forgave? How did you feel emotionally and physically? How did the act of forgiveness impact your life? Pay attention to stories of forgiveness as you go through the day—you may hear more than you expect.

- **Ask yourself, "Who do I need to forgive?"** Now see that child of God in your mind's eye. Recognize that his or her actions and your reaction came from fear, which has no power in the face of love. Ask Spirit to heal any resistance that you have to forgiving. Then say the words, "I forgive you" as though he or she was standing right in front of you. Take a deep breath and feel the peace of Self-love. Finally, before you go to sleep tonight, ask for the soothing and rest that forgiveness offers, and give thanks for answered prayers.

❈ **Identify a grievance that you hold against someone as a result of something he or she did or said.** Now, instead of focusing on the actions, look inside and ask yourself these questions:

How did my ego use the other person's words or actions to reinforce a fear in myself?

Does that person's actions in any way change the fact that I am love and light?

Do this with thoughtful intention, asking for help and understanding from Spirit. As any feelings come up, let yourself feel them, and remember these words from *A Course in Miracles:* "Forgiveness always rests upon the one who offers it."

What does true forgiveness look like in action?

I. **A friend of yours, who happens to be on vacation, comments on your Facebook post, insinuating that you're a messy housekeeper.** The arrow hit its target, and you feel vulnerable, hurt, and blindsided.

If you don't practice true forgiveness, your ego will go into attack mode and plan ways to retaliate or punish your friend. "She'll never hear from *me* again," it might say. "Maybe I'll unfriend her. Or ignore all her posts. Or throw it back in her face and tell her I'll never invite her to our house again if that's how she feels about it." Go, ego, go. Nothing is accomplished except the end of a friendship.

If you do practice true forgiveness, you'll forgive yourself for a lack of Self-love. Your friend's comments will bounce off of you because you aren't judging yourself for your own housekeeping. There is no attack, and the comments aren't about you. There's nothing to forgive. You might, however, want to find out what's going on with your friend. If she spends her vacation posting hurtful comments, she might be issuing a call for love.

2. You're walking with your African-American cousin and a man drives up, stops, and yells, "Go back to Africa where you belong!" Your cousin is shocked and doesn't know what to say. Your ego is immediately triggered and wants to hurl insults—if not rocks—at the driver. Instead, you take a breath, look him in the eye, and say, "Sir, whatever or whoever made you feel that way, I'm really sorry. I wish you all the best." Then you both walk away and send him love.

Or, better yet, you look him in the eye and say, "Hey, do you know where the local bakery is? I've heard this town has some great Dutch pastries."

I'm not kidding.

His words were egregious, but he was talking to himself and trying to make your cousin the target of his own self-loathing. The situation only has meaning if you pick up a sword and fall into line on the battleground. But when you rise above, you remove the target and neutralize his attack. He might as well have said, "Nice weather we're having."

Given that, changing the subject can be an appropriate response. It brightens the light in you. And you never know. When you ask him to help you, your request might remind him that there's light under his darkness.

3. A child is abused by her uncle and tells her mother. The mom doesn't believe her, and the child blames herself. It takes years before she can sort out the feelings of betrayal, abandonment, and self-loathing.

But think of how things change if the child's mom believes her, alerts the authorities, practices true forgiveness, and talks with the girl.

"I'm so sorry he did this to you," she might say. "What he did was very wrong. He's sick, and the authorities will get him some help. And I'd like for us to see a counselor who can help you talk about your feelings, too. I want you to know that what he did was not because of you. Sometimes when people hurt inside, they hurt others. I'm sorry you were the one involved. I think it's important for us to forgive him so we won't build our lives around the hurt."

Now, I'm not saying this is easy. I know many, many women—and men—who have been sexually assaulted as children or adults. And I fully understand how much the ego wants to demand justice. But I've also seen that holding onto the anger is every bit as hurtful as the original abuse— sometimes even more so. Not just because it perpetuates the pain, but because it keeps you locked behind the bars of fear, and you can never fully experience what you are.

Making a perpetrator into a monster and condemning him gives momentary relief. But then the healing work must begin. That process is always about Self-love, the essential element of true forgiveness.

———

In these days of noisy voices that demand retribution and revenge, quiet stories of forgiveness often are overlooked. But we need them to show us that true forgiveness is not only possible, it's the natural order of things when we practice Self-love, seeing with the eyes of Spirit and honoring our unity.

This is what true forgiveness can sound like:

❁ "I'm not giving it another thought. I hope you won't either."

❁ "I think every situation is an opportunity to learn. Thank you for being my teacher."

❁ "I wouldn't have chosen this situation, but now I'm grateful we went through it together."

- ❋ "I know you were operating from your own fears, and I took that hurt personally. I've had similar fears and might have done the same thing in your shoes."

- ❋ "I see the light in you. No matter what has happened between us, I know that light is as strong as ever."

Remember: Forgiveness is not just letting someone off the hook, denying your own feelings of anger or betrayal. Forgiveness is choosing the higher Self's peace over the ego's need to be right.

And as *A Course in Miracles* says, if you want peace, forgiveness is the path. It will lead you to freedom, which is our final principle.

ten

Set Your Self Free

So here we are at the end—or maybe it's the beginning. The ten principles in this book are cumulative, but they're also part of the same whole. Alpha and omega, a representation of the infinite light within.

The truth is, you will continue to learn and grow not in a straight line, but in a spiral of ever-rising and evolving knowledge and awakening. Often you'll feel as though you're holding the answers in your hand, only to drop them and wonder if they rolled under the couch or dropped into a black hole.

But then, right in the middle of a gripe session at work or the stress of sitting in heavy traffic, one of these principles will float in, reminding you of the light that you are.

My friend Judy calls this "flickering enlightenment," the three-steps-forward-two-steps-back process that eventually leads to true freedom.

But what does that mean? What would real freedom look and feel like to you?

—

As I write this book, I'm recovering from a kidney stone that presented itself in the middle of the night. My husband, Bob, fell on the ice a week ago and landed on his back, so he's been sore. A friend has a brain tumor. Another is going through radiation for breast cancer.

The situation in North Korea seems unpredictable. Gang members are causing near riots downtown. And I'm sitting in our living room with a roll of toilet paper so I can periodically pick boxelder bugs off our windows and flush them down the toilet because they like to come in the house and die.

Also in my life right now, robins have returned for the spring. Most of our friends and family are physically healthy. We get to do work that we love. We look out over rolling hills every day. We're expecting a new grandchild this year. The world is filled with kind and compassionate people.

This is a normal day. It's probably no worse or better than yours.

These are the things that are happening around me, in the external world. But most of the time, what's going on inside is pretty peaceful, whether I'm focused on the future grandbaby or the political races. And I don't say that because I'm special. I'm saying it because I marvel at what's possible for all of us: to live in a peaceful world no matter what is happening around us, because we are the light and have peace within.

This is true freedom.

Getting there doesn't mean withdrawing from the world, shaking our heads, and washing our hands of it. This is about being *in* the world, actively engaged, but carrying the peace inside ourselves into that world so we can be part of the change.

That's why this book is called *Be the Light that You Are.* It's an imperative. You *are* the light, now *be* that light in the world. Don't ignore that part of yourself. Don't be falsely humble and pretend that you're not good enough. Don't buy into the collective "I don't matter."

If you had a gift as a concert pianist, you wouldn't hide it. You'd perform so others could be inspired and uplifted by the beauty of your music. If you were a gifted surgeon, you wouldn't pretend your skills didn't matter. You'd use them to heal people.

So why, when you have light within you, would you hide it and not use it in the world? It's a tool. It's what we need. And we need it from *you*. In fact, we need it *now*.

If you bring peace to the world rather than try to find peace in the world, you will change the world.

If you bring love to the world rather than try to find love in the world, you will change the world.

If you bring acceptance to the world rather than try to find acceptance in the world, you will change the world.

That's why it starts with you, and why it's so essential to be the light that you are. That's where the peace comes from. Not *from* you but *through* you. That's your assignment.

So no excuses. No more delays.

Being the light means moving the world forward with love rather than fear. As *A Course in Miracles* says, "Seek not to change the world, but choose to change your mind about the world." This starts with you living out the inner peace that's inside you. Feeling the freedom to be the light that you are.

⌐

Here are effective ways to set yourself free.

Engage in acts of kindness. They matter. They're more than cumulative because they remind us who we are as the light, and that light can have unexpectedly broad results.

Hitler, for instance, was one small man in one small country who used fear to build an empire that could not

"Being the light means moving the world forward with love rather than fear. And it starts with you living out the inner peace that's inside you."

stand the test of time. Look at the loss of life, all the despair and heartbreak that came from one person because people listened to the voice of fear rather than their higher Self, the voice of love. Fear is loud and insistent in the external world. And it is loud and insistent in your own mind.

But if you let it run your life, you're building an empire of despair just as Hitler did. People ask, "Why didn't anyone stop him?" But the better question is, "Why do we persist in building empires of hate, persecution, judgment, and attack in our own ego minds?" Hitler was not an aberration. He was enabled by the fear in all of us. It's time for this to stop, but it must stop with each of us.

That's why we can never underestimate the power of an act of compassion or kindness. There's evidence of at least one school shooting being prevented when a student reached out in kindness, not knowing that his simple act made an angry and isolated young man feel like he belonged.

Similarly, I know someone who was planning an ambush when, out of the blue, he received a text from an old friend. The message reminded him of his greater purpose, and as a result, he put his gun down.

And I know a family that was fractured over one person's alcoholism, but came back together when one of them simply said, "How can I help?"

The examples of kindnesses interrupting attacks and suicides, or simply brightening someone's day, are countless. So if you feel overwhelmed and think you can't make a difference, just reach out in one small way. Your simple act could change the course of history.

Hand everything over to the Holy Spirit. Recently, my ego mind clearly wanted attention, so it started chewing on a question about my next book. Did I have the right topic? Was I interviewing the right people? Had I started a list to keep track of possible titles?

Control, control, control. This inner ego fest didn't go on long before I asked for my fear-based thoughts to be healed and said to myself and Spirit, "I'm *so* happy I don't need to have the answers."

With that statement, peace settled over me. I felt carefree, the way I did when I was a kid and had no real responsibilities. My only job was to enjoy the moment, trusting that Spirit would take care of things. Total freedom.

And that's exactly what *A Course in Miracles* advises us to do: Ask the Holy Spirit for help with *everything*. No exceptions.

Somehow, in some way, I totally missed that message for, oh . . . the first twenty-five years I studied the *Course*.

That's how much my ego did *not* want me to rely on the Holy Spirit. And it's the reason I want to be sure *you* don't miss the message.

Ask Spirit for help. Ask Spirit for help. In everything you do, ask Spirit for help.

Contrary to what your ego would have you believe, He has time for you, you matter to Him, and you are completely worthy of His attention.

Plus, to the Holy Spirit, the difference between love and fear is simple to see. He's not confused by shades of gray.

So let's say you got into an argument with your best friend. She keeps breaking lunch dates, and she wasn't there for you when your son broke his arm.

In your mind, you're reliving the whole thing over and over. "We used to be so close. What's gotten into her? Was I too hard on her? Did I let her off too easy? Is this all my fault? Am I the worst friend ever?"

You get the idea. The ego takes hold of the issue like a dog with a rag bone, shaking it right and left and working itself into a frenzy by using all its tricks.

Anger. Guilt. Blame. Living in the past. Living in the future.

So how does the Holy Spirit undo this tangled mess the ego has made?

He says, "All is well. You're a holy child of God. So is your friend. Let me take care of the rest."

That's it. He doesn't care what either of you did yesterday or three years ago, or what you're going to do tomorrow. He looks at this moment, and this one, and this one. And He reminds you that nothing has changed. You're still love.

As you go through your day, become aware of when you start to get aggravated, frustrated, or afraid. When you do, stop and ask the Holy Spirit to heal your fear-based thoughts. And feel free to ask *many* times through the day. If in doubt, simply say, "Help!" Then pay attention to the freedom you feel.

Trust the power of prayer. Here's what *A Course in Miracles* says about prayers being answered: "The very fact that the Holy Spirit has been asked for anything will ensure a response. Yet it is equally certain that no response given by Him will ever be one that would increase fear. It is possible that His answer will not be heard. It is impossible, however, that it will be lost. There are many answers you have already received but have not yet heard. I assure you that they are waiting for you."

So, if I'm thinking my prayers aren't being answered, I can correctly say to the Holy Spirit, "It's not you. It's me."

I may have prayed earnestly for what I consider the perfect new job. But if I'm not ready for it, that prayer can't be answered . . . yet.

I may long for a life partner, but if I have work to do in loving my Self, the Holy Spirit will help me with that issue first before bringing the right person into my life.

I may pray to lose weight. But if I subconsciously fear that a slimmer me would be ostracized by my family—who all equate food with love—the Holy Spirit can't yet help those pounds disappear.

This is why it's essential to ask for fears to be healed, because that healing clears the path for our prayers to be answered.

Think of something you've prayed for that hasn't yet shown up.

Maybe you have been mad at God or the Holy Spirit for dropping the ball or withholding it from you. Maybe it has made you doubt your faith altogether.

Whatever it is, write it down or draw a picture of it so you can look at it, right in front of you. Now ask yourself, "What am I afraid of? What fear in me needs to be healed so this prayer can be answered? Am I asking for what I truly want?"

Talk to the Holy Spirit about it, and be open to any guidance you receive.

Then give thanks for answered—or unanswered—prayers.

Help one person and know that you may be helped by someone completely different. Forgive one and be forgiven by another. This is important because it frees you—and everyone else—to give and receive without expectations of reciprocity.

Ask yourself: What's right with this picture? Let's say you've been feeling low on energy for a while and can't seem to shake it. All you want to do is rest, read, and catch up on Netflix.

Or let's say you've been pretty social most of your life, but lately you'd rather spend time in your garden.

Or maybe you've typically dated quiet types, and all of a sudden you find yourself enjoying the company of a real extrovert instead.

Your ego is likely to ask, "What's wrong with this picture?" It will assume that, if something has changed, it's a sign of trouble—even if you're more peaceful and happier than ever.

So here's a different question you could ask the Holy Spirit: "What's right with this picture?"

Maybe the need for rest signals that a new idea is being born in you, or your higher Self is asking for quiet time to reflect on a big decision you're facing.

Maybe the desire for less people time and more garden time means you're getting more grounded.

Maybe the change in the type of person you're dating shows a shift from special relationships to holy ones.

Maybe—just maybe—the Holy Spirit can help you see the changes through the lens of love rather than fear.

That's the great thing about talking with the Holy Spirit often. You get a different perspective, reassurance, and a reminder that all is well.

For today, whenever you start to think something is wrong in your life, stop and ask the Holy Spirit, "What's right with this picture?"

Stop fighting and let your Self be loved. Think of a horse that gets caught in barbed wire. The more it fights and flails, the more pain it will inflict on itself. Our ego minds are like the horse, trying to get free of the pain. But when we can sit still and ask for help from Spirit, we minimize our own suffering. Your spiritual helpers will be with you, lifting you above the perils of your own ego mind if you allow them to.

Remember: Reacting to life differently than you have in the past requires a different perspective. A fresh way of looking at things. A new application of love. And it's the only way the cycle of anger and guilt and attack will end. Long term, it's the only thing that works. So if you feel trapped in fear, see yourself putting peace in a box, gift wrapping it, and handing it to someone—or maybe to your Self. This simple act will remind you who and what you are, which is always where your freedom lies.

In every chapter of this book, I've included examples to illustrate what the principles look like in action. This time, though, I'd like to share something from my own life that I hope will have value for you.

It's a commitment I wrote to myself a year ago. I read it often. In fact, I could benefit from reading it every day.

It incorporates all the principles we've talked about, and it demonstrates my desire to live them in every area of my life.

Do I always succeed? No. But putting these intentions in writing and revisiting them frequently helps affirm the life that I know is possible. This written commitment is not a cause to berate myself when my ego takes over. Instead, it's a roadmap to help me stay on track or regain my footing when I take a fear-based detour.

The more I spend time with these affirmations, the more my life moves in the direction of peace.

They remind me of all the blessings in my life so I don't take them for granted. They comfort me in knowing that Spirit is always here guiding and supporting me. And they help me remember the light that I am.

I encourage you to write something similar for yourself, to update it when you need to, and to spend time with it every day.

So here it is, the sum total of our ten principles, shared with my greatest blessings to you.

⁓

Like everyone in this world, I am a perfect expression of God's love and divine light. Nothing can change that, but I sometimes forget. When I do, I know I'm not broken, lost, or alone. All I have to do is ask for help from Spirit and remember what I am.

Our home extends love to everyone who enters. It's a place of welcome, where we honor the light in others and help them celebrate it in themselves. Like all of us, it is perfect in its quirks and imperfections, providing a safe harbor for laughter, comfort, acceptance, respite, and forgiveness.

I send blessings to everyone on the planet—all the friends and family who share the riches of lifelong relationship, all the people who have enriched my life with their unique gifts, and all the people I may never meet but are part of my human family.

I send love, healing, and peace to places of conflict around the world. I know this energy will be carried by the Holy Spirit exactly where it needs to go to transform fear into love.

I send my husband deep appreciation and love for our commitment to one another. I thank him for his kindness, his friendship, and his steadfastness, and for all the growth we've experienced with one another.

When my ego pulls me into discouragement or worry, I ask to be lifted above the battleground where I can see through a new lens, through spiritual eyes. From this vantage point, I know my mind can help find peaceful and creative solutions in every situation.

I surrender my ego's need to control, fix, or interfere so I can let everyone in my life be who and what they are. I realize I can't see the bigger picture, and that any judgment on my part is based on my own insecurities and limited information. And so I lovingly detach, trusting that everything is working for the highest good and asking for my words and actions to be motivated by love.

I know that life is not lived in the past or the future, and I'm reminded every day to focus on possibilities unfolding in this very moment. I forgive myself and everyone else for hurts that have come from fear, and I ask for all our hearts to be healed so we can start fresh with one another every single day.

I am infinitely grateful for the exquisite tenderness, beauty, and strength in this world, and for the eternal flame that shines in all of us.

In love, we bring healing to Earth.
In unity, we live in peace.
In light, we remember what we are.
I say thank you, and Amen.

About the Author

PHOTO BY AMY ALLEN

Debra Landwehr Engle is the author of *The Only Little Prayer You Need*, *Let Your Spirit Guides Speak*, and *Grace from the Garden*. Cofounder of a women's program of spiritual growth, she also is a long-time student and teacher of *A Course in Miracles*.

A speaker and workshop facilitator, Debra works with individuals on personal growth and writing through one-on-one mentoring, online programs, and international retreats.

She lives with her husband Bob in Madison County, Iowa, home of the famed covered bridges.

You can visit her at *www.debraengle.com*.

Hampton Roads Publishing Company

. . . *for the evolving human spirit*

Hampton Roads Publishing Company publishes books on a variety of subjects, including spirituality, health, and other related topics.

For a copy of our latest trade catalog, call (978) 465-0504 or visit our distributor's website at *www.redwheelweiser.com*. You can also sign up for our newsletter and special offers by going to *www.redwheelweiser.com/newsletter/*.